· GOLD ·

LIBERTY
1854

GOLD

The Fascinating Story of the Noble Metal Through the Ages

DANIEL COHEN

M. EVANS AND COMPANY, INC. / NEW YORK, N.Y. 10017

To Henry Morrison

M. Evans and Company titles are distributed in the United States by the J. B. Lippincott Company, East Washington Square, Philadelphia, Pa. 19105; and in Canada by McClelland & Stewart Ltd., 25 Hollinger Road, Toronto M4B 3G2, Ontario

LIBRARY OF CONGRESS CATALOGING IN PUBLICATION DATA

Cohen, Daniel.
Gold: the fascinating story of the noble metal through the ages.

Bibliography: p.
Includes index.
SUMMARY: Discusses gold, a valuable metal which has influenced history from the Egyptians to the present.
1. Gold—Juvenile literature. [1. Gold] I. Title.
HG289.C63 332.4'222'09 76-18067
ISBN 0-87131-218-2

Design by Joel Schick

Manufactured in the United States of America

9 8 7 6 5 4 3 2 1

CONTENTS

1

THE NOBLE METAL

Ask for a scientific definition of gold and you will get something like this:

> Gold is an element that is one of the hundred or so fundamental substances in the universe that are composed of atoms of only one kind. Its chemical symbol is Au, an abbreviation for *aurum,* the Latin word for gold. It is a nonferrous metal, with an atomic number of 79 and an atomic weight of 196-.967. It has a specific gravity of 19.32. Its melting

OPPOSITE: *Funeral mask of Tut-ankh-amun, made of solid gold.* (Photo by Harry Burton, The Metropolitan Museum of Art)

> point is fairly low for a metal, 1,063 degrees Celsius or 1,945 degrees Fahrenheit. Gold boils at 2,966 degrees Celsius.

While such a definition may mean a great deal to a scientist, it doesn't really mean a great deal to you and me. The one thing that we all know about gold is that it is extremely valuable. In recent years the price of gold has fluctuated a lot, but it has generally hovered between one hundred and two hundred dollars an ounce. One ounce of pure gold is about the size of a half-dollar.

Gold is clearly an expensive metal, but merely quoting the price does not adequately describe the value that we place on gold. Only experienced goldworkers and, one imagines, the very, very rich can stand near a large quantity of gold without feeling a bit awed by it. We feel ourselves to be in the presence of something more than just an expensive metal. In the past, gold has had great religious significance. It is no exaggeration to say that gold retains a semi-religious significance in the modern world.

Sometimes financial authorities try to describe gold as "another commodity," a material that is bought and sold like barrels of oil or bushels of wheat. We can't run a car on gold, and we can't eat it either, yet it can touch our deepest emotions in a way that oil and grain and other commodities can not.

In addition to being valuable, gold is also very pretty. Oil is downright ugly, and the best thing that one can say about the appearance of wheat is that its color is "golden." Pure gold possesses a rich yellow color. In the light it appears to shine brightly with a warm orange-red glow. Of course, gold doesn't have any light of its own; the secret of its brightness is its ability to reflect light.

Many metals are highly reflective when polished, but one of the most remarkable things about gold is that it never loses its brightness. This quality of gold is called nobility and that is no mere flight of poetic fancy either. Technically, nobility means that gold does not react with oxygen, and therefore will not rust like iron or corrode like copper. What is more, gold resists the action of most acids.

Imagine a treasure ship sunk to the bottom of the sea. The timbers of the ship will rot, and the guns rust or corrode. The chests in which the gold was stored will fall to pieces in just a few years. But the gold itself will remain completely unaffected by hundreds of years of immersion in salt water. Bring it to the surface, clean off the accumulated debris of the sea, and the gold will be just as bright as it ever was.

Gold can be repeatedly melted and remelted without damaging the material itself in any way. It can be fashioned into a piece of jewelry, thrown back into the melting pot, cast into a ingot, melted again, stamped into a coin, and so on. Historically, this has been the fate of most gold. The low melting point of gold makes its reuse an easy task. Gold is as close to an immortal substance as we are ever likely to encounter.

As a result, virtually every bit of gold that has ever been mined or picked up since man first became interested in the shiny yellow metal is still around somewhere in some form or other. A modern wedding band, or even a gold tooth filling may contain gold that at one time was part of the death mask of an Egyptian Pharoah, a decoration in an Incan temple, a coin from the mints of Croesus of Lydia, or a pirate's treasure. That notion might sound a bit romantic, because the majority of gold that has ever been mined has been mined within the last century. But, romantic or not, it is still possible.

If you have a chance to hold a gold bar of any size at all, you will find that it is very heavy, probably heavier than you expected it to be. Gold is one of the heaviest of the metals. It weighs 19.32 times the weight of its own volume in water. That is what a specific gravity of 19.32 means.

For all its weight, gold is also surprisingly soft. If the gold bar you hold is one of great purity, you should be able to mark its surface with your fingernail. This extreme softness of gold has both advantages and drawbacks. Jewelry made from what is called ultrapure gold would quickly show signs of wear. Most gold is alloyed with other metals—usually copper, nickel, or silver—which make it harder, but do not detract from the beauty of the material. Just a tiny quantity of alloy will give gold a much harder finish.

When we speak of gold being so many carats, we are speaking of the purity of the gold. Originally, carats were a measure of weight, used primarily in the gem trade. But in the case of gold carats have nothing to do with weight. Pure gold is defined as twenty-four-carat gold. Eighteen-carat gold is 18/24 gold or three-quarters gold. The fewer carats, the smaller the percentage of gold. Most of the gold that one is likely to encounter in jewelry or coins is less than twenty-four carats. When you get into the range of nine-carat gold, it is questionable if the material should be properly called gold at all, since more than half of it is something else.

Pure, or near-pure gold, is generally seen only in ingots that are used as the raw material for a jewelry maker, or stored in a bank. Even pure gold is less than 100 percent gold. Most of the gold that enters the market is between 99.5 and 99.9 percent pure. A tiny quantity of copper, nickel, silver, or other metal can be found in all commercial gold.

The softness or malleability of gold is also a characteristic that has made the metal extremely useful. It has allowed artisans and jewelers to shape gold into an almost endless variety of elaborate and often exquisite forms, and they were able to do so without advanced technology.

The half-dollar-sized ounce of gold can be hammered into a thin sheet covering one hundred square feet. Very thin sheets of beaten gold, called gold leaf, have been used to cover the domes of churches and the roofs of palaces; and gold leaf was used to decorate books and manuscripts. Modern technology makes it possible to stretch gold even farther. An ounce of gold can be drawn into a wire fifty miles long, or used to plate one thousand miles of fine copper wire.

Because gold can be spread so thinly, we might get the impression that there is more gold available than is actually the case. It has been estimated that if all the gold mined since the beginning of time were melted into gold bars and stacked in one place, these bars could be piled into a cube with sides a little over fifty feet square. The mass of gold would weigh about eighty thousand metric tons, but it would easily fit within the limits of a baseball diamond.

Though by any measure gold is an exceedingly rare metal, it is somewhat more common on earth than the figures of the gold mined by man would suggest. Traces of gold have been found in all parts of the globe; however, its appearance in commercially usable quantities is an event rare enough to set off a gold rush. Every ton of earth is likely to contain a few pennies worth of gold, but it would cost many dollars to extract that gold.

Gold can even be found in sea water, though there is only about one part gold to six hundred million parts of water. Still, given the amount of water in the sea, the amount of gold locked up in it is impressive. Getting gold out of sea water is one of those ideas that seem to hold an endless fascination for inventors. Over fifty schemes designed to extract gold from sea water have been patented. Technically, extracting gold from sea is possible, but the processes that have been suggested cost far more than the recovered gold could ever conceivably be worth.

When the earth was formed, gold, being one of the heavier metals, tended to be concentrated in the planet's interior. Thus, there is more gold far beneath the surface of the earth than there is on or near the surface. At one time there was a theory that the earth's core was pure gold. It isn't. Even at the center of the earth, gold is a relatively scarce element and only a small percentage of the earth's core is gold. The core of the earth is predominantely nickel and iron.

A few years back Dr. Harrison Brown of the University of Chicago Institute for Nuclear Studies tried to figure out how much gold we might obtain if we could mine deep within the earth's interior. He estimated that if it were possible to sink a hole fifteen hundred to two thousand miles into the earth, we could get enough gold to plate the surface of our planet to a depth of several yards.

But wresting gold from the earth's core may be an impossible dream (and an unnecessary one, for there is no particular reason to have that much gold in circulation). Currently the deepest gold mine is a little more than two miles. Even at that comparatively modest depth, the pressure on the rock of the roof of the mine is tremendous, and this makes the always hazardous task of mining infinitely more at a risk. In the late 1960s there was a well-publicized attempt to drill a hole through the earth's core to the underlying mantle of the earth, a paltry six miles. The project ran into enormous technical and financial problems and was finally abandoned.

Future space travelers might expect to find gold on the inner planets, Mercury, Venus, and Mars, for they, along with the earth, are the smallest and densest of the planets. The outer planets are not thought to contain any gold.

As we already noted, when the earth was formed, the gold and other heavy elements collected in the center. Most of the gold that lodged there eons ago is still there today—but not all of it. The molten interior of the earth exerts a constant pressure on the outlying crust upon which we live. Sometimes this pressure results in spectacular volcanic explosions. The pressure also crumbles the crust, creating mountain ranges. It breaks the earth's crust along fault lines that are prey to earthquakes, and probably even moves continents around. These geological processes are exceedingly slow in terms of a human lifespan, but they have been going on for a very long time. As a result, much material from the center of the earth has been pushed to or near the surface.

The heat and chemical reactions involved in mountain building may, under particular conditions, concentrate widely distributed gold in certain rocks. If the concentration is high enough, these gold-bearing rocks are worth mining. In nature, though, gold is rarely found in a pure or near-pure state. It is usually alloyed with silver or other metals. In South Africa, where most of the world's gold is mined today, the ore occurs as streaks in quartz rock. Most gold ore does not gleam yellow as does refined gold. It takes an expert to recognize even the richest of ore-bearing rocks. You or I could look at a piece of ore from a gold mine without having the faintest notion of what it was. The ore must be crushed and processed before the yellow metal can be extracted from it.

If all gold could be found only in this form, it would have been a long time before it was recognized, and gold would probably never have played so important a part in world history for so long. But, occasionally, gold naturally occurs in pure or nearly pure form, and then it is easily recognizable.

Mountains that were formed eons ago have gradually been worn away by the action of wind, water, weather, and the roots of plants. The heavier gold-bearing rocks may be separated from the lighter barren material and exposed on the surface by erosion. Sometimes the gold is washed into riverbeds, where it settles as dust or as larger chunks called nuggets. A gold nugget about the size of a pea set off the great California gold rush of 1849. The largest gold nugget ever found was the Welcome Stranger, a 2,280-ounce chunk of near-pure gold that was discovered near Moligul in the Australian province of Victoria in 1869.

Gold is rarely so easy to come by.

2

ANCIENT GOLD

We will never know where gold was first considered something special, or why. The earliest evidence we have of systematic mining and working of gold comes from Egypt. We know for certain that from the very beginning of their long history the Egyptians had a high regard for gold, and they developed unparalleled skills in working with the metal. The skills that the Egyptians pioneered influenced other civilizations of the ancient Middle East, and ultimately of the whole world. Even if

PPOSITE: *Stylized 5th century Sythian reindeer pendants of solid old.* (The Metropolitan Museum of Art, Fletcher Fund, 1924)

gold was not used first in Egypt, Egypt was the gateway through which all the early techniques and beliefs about gold passed, and were transformed. And so the story of gold must start in Egypt, the land of the Nile River.

Why did the Egyptians first begin to value gold so highly? We can only guess, for the records from very early times are either sketchy or nonexistent. But it appears that it was the color of gold that first brought it to the attention of the people of Egypt, for its color is like that of the sun. In the dry and cloudless climate of Egypt, the sun is an overpowering, omnipresent fact of life. In one sense or another, the ancient Egyptians always worshipped the sun, identifying it with their chief god, Ra. So it seems logical to conclude that the sun-colored metal, gold, would have been identified with the sun's divine qualities.

Some six thousand years ago, before Egypt was even a unified country, the people at a place now called El Gerza, a little south of modern Cairo, were making necklaces and earrings from the gold they found in the sands of the Nile River. A king called Narmer, who is generally credited with having welded Egypt into a single nation, also minted standard-sized gold bars stamped with his seal. (These may have been used as money.)

Removing gold from alluvial sand is a tedious process of repeatedly washing the sand to separate the gold dust from it. Often it also involved digging through the surface silt, to richer gold deposits below. But the shafts never had to be very deep. Most alluvial gold was found in the Nile sands of Nubia, south of Egypt. *Nub* was the Egyptian word for gold.

Not all Egyptian gold came from the Nile, however.

Gold was also discovered on the plateau between the Nile and the Red Sea. The first of this plateau gold was found on the surface, but that supply was soon exhausted, and the Egyptians had to dig for more. The remains of these ancient mines still exist, their underground tunnels stretching for miles. Most of the digging was done with pickaxes, first made of bronze and then of iron. It was hideous work.

Diodorus, a Greek philosopher writing in the second century B.C., described the conditions in the Egyptian gold mines. "The king of Egypt consigned to the gold mines those who had been condemned for crimes and who had been made captive in war . . . many in number and all bound with fetters."

Theophrastus, another Greek philosopher of about the same period, supplied details:

> Those who dig in the mines cannot stand upright at their work, but are obliged to lie down, either on their back or on their side, for the vein of earth they dig runs lengthwise and is only the depth of two feet though considerably more in breadth, and it is enclosed on every side with hard rock from which the ore is obtained.

After the ore-bearing rock was hacked from the earth, it was pounded and ground to powder fineness. The powdered ore was then spread on sloping boards and water was continually poured over it until the heavier gold was separated from the lighter material.

Most of Egypt's gold came from the sands of Nubia or the plateau of the Red Sea, but it also seems likely that some gold was imported from elsewhere. In the records of Queen Hatshepsut, that truly remarkable woman who ruled Egypt during the time of its greatest glory, there is description of the return of a trading expedition from a land called Punt. It has long been thought that Punt was a source of Egyptian gold, but unfortunately no one knows what part of the world the Egyptians called Punt. Yet, the merest hint that this land had contained gold has caused explorers and travelers to "locate" it everywhere from the southern tip of Africa to Syria. In fact, no one knows where Punt was, or if it ever contained any gold.

Gold is too soft a metal to make useful tools or weapons, and too heavy to make convenient pots. What then did the Egyptians want all that gold for? They wanted it for the same reason that many want gold today, for ornamentation. Early in Egyptian history the goldsmiths learned how to sheathe wood and metal objects with gold. They would cast gold, draw it into fine wires or beat it into paper-thin sheets. Egyptian artisans could cover a piece of jewelry with hundreds of tiny gold granules and decorate it with turquoise or other precious and semiprecious stones. In short, until comparatively recent times most of the goldworking techniques known to man were used by the ancient Egyptians.

The wealthy, both men and women, festooned themselves with golden ornaments. Egypt's innumerable temples also received a generous share of gold. But surely the most lavish user of gold in Egypt was the king or Pharoah. As a living, visible representative of the divine presence, it must have seemed only natural for the Pharoah to appear before his people arrayed in the golden splendor of the sun. He sat on a throne sheathed with gold, wore a golden headdress, and a golden collar. His sandals were golden. Even the false beard he often wore was made of gold. The great Queen Hatshepsut is also shown wearing a golden beard on ceremonial occasions.

The golden array of a living Pharoah, however, was far surpassed by the amount of gold consumed for the burial of a dead Pharoah. We have all heard of pyramids and mummies and of the treasures buried in the tombs of the Pharoahs. As a result there is a popular image of ancient Egypt as a morbid, death-centered society. That was not the case at all. The Egyptians were a vigorous people who loved life and expected all that was good in this life to continue in the next. That gave them a considerably more cheerful view of the world beyond the grave than that of most peoples, ancient or modern.

In their long history, the Egyptians developed an astonishing collection of religious and magical techniques, aimed at assuring a happy life in the next world. One of them involved burying the dead with a great deal of treasure. In the case of the Pharoahs the amount of treasure interred with the mummy is mind-boggling, and most of that treasure was gold. The permanence of gold must have made it very attractive for funerary goods. So much effort was expended on preserving the corpse for eternity, it must have appeared logical to supply the corpse with as much of this eternal metal as possible. The analogy of the incorruptible metal and the immortal spirit would not have been lost on the Egyptians, who found much meaning in analogy.

A modern glimpse of the splendor of the tombs of the Pharoahs came in 1922 when archaeologists led by the Englishman Howard Carter discovered the essentially unplundered tomb of Pharoah Tutankhamen. Tutankhamen was one of the least glorious kings in Egypt's history. He died young, after a short undistinguished reign. Many of the furnishings in his tomb had originally been used for the tomb of one of his predecessors, but had been snatched by Tutankhamen during a period of political and religious turmoil. His tomb could in no sense rival those of the truly great Pharoahs. And yet, what golden treasures it held!

Aside from the innumerable objects made of gold or covered and inlaid with gold, there was the final resting place of Tutankhamen's mummy itself. The mummy was encased within four burial shrines of gilded wood. Inside the shrines were three coffins, the first two of wood covered by gold leaf, the third of solid gold. This third coffin contained close to twenty-five hundred pounds of pure gold. And even that was not enough, for when the golden coffin was opened it revealed an extraordinary gold death mask, a striking portrait of the dead king. The mask is now considered one of the greatest golden treasures ever found.

Ironically, the mummy itself, which all this costly panoply had been designed to protect was in terrible shape. The priests had poured on an excess of oils that were supposed to preserve the body of the king. The result was that the mummy was practically embedded in a black tarlike mass. Archaeologists, even with the most careful attention, were able to salvage very little of it. But the gold was as good as it had ever been.

Yet, the very gold that was meant to assure the immortality of the Pharoahs certainly helped to assure the destruction of their tombs. Tutankhamen was the only

Pharoah whose tomb remained unplundered until modern times. Most of the royal Egyptian tombs, including the pyramids, were plundered in ancient times, perhaps only a few years or decades after they were sealed.

Reflecting on the riches he had uncovered, archaeologist Howard Carter wrote:

> How great must have been the wealth buried with those ancient Pharoahs! What riches that valley [the Valley of the Kings] must have once concealed! Of the twenty-seven monarchs buried there, Tutankhamen was probably of the least importance. How great must have been the temptation to the greed and rapacity of the audacious contemporary tomb robbers! What stronger incentive can be imagined than those vast treasures of gold!

There was evidence that thieves had made a raid on Tutankhamen's tomb, but for some reason abandoned the effort before they had gotten very far. The tomb was then resealed and forgotten.

The tomb robbers were often aided and protected by corrupt local officials and priests. It is probable that many Pharoahs also stole the treasures of their predecessors for their own greater glory. Tutankhamen certainly did this, and later monarchs from all parts of the world became adept at the practice.

The result is that very little of what once must have been an enormous quantity of Egyptian golden artistry survives. Most of it had been melted down centuries ago.

Why would a robber bother to melt down such treasures? Obviously, the value of an object such as the death mask of Tutankhamen, is to us, far, far greater than the value of the unworked gold or bullion from which it is made.

But we cannot be sure that the ancients held the same values. To an Egyptian, obtaining gold with which to make objects for his own tomb may have been more important than obtaining a golden object from someone else's tomb, no matter how well made it might have been. What is art when compared with immortality?

There is an even more persuasive reason. Golden objects are potentially traceable, gold bars are not. This same knowledge has dominated the actions of tomb robbers, and other robbers of gold as well, for thousands of years, and for this reason only a tiny fraction of the golden treasures of the past have escaped the melting pot.

The Egyptians were well aware of the use of gold as a diplomatic weapon. Hostile neighbors could be made less hostile, and friendly neighbors kept friendly with generous gifts of gold. In short, gold could be used as a bribe, and there was no shame in it. When one Burnaburiash, ruler of a minor kingdom to the north of Egypt, felt that he had not received sufficient gold, he complained about it in no uncertain terms in a letter to the Pharaoh:

> All goes well for me. All hail to thee, thy house, thy wives, thy children, thy country, thy nobles, thy horses and thy chariots.
>
> When my fathers and thy fathers established between themselves friendly relations they exchanged rich presents and never refused each other, the

> one to the other, whatever beautiful thing they desired.
> Now my brother has sent me as a gift but two minas of gold [about twenty-five ounces]. If now gold is abundant with thee, send me as much as thy fathers did, but if it is scarce, send me at least half as much. Why didst thou send me only two minas of gold? . . . Send me much gold.

The Pharaoh's reply, if any, has not survived.

While the Egyptians may have been the earliest workers of gold, and quite possibly the ancient world's most skilled and lavish users of gold, they certainly were not the only ones. The second most celebrated archaeological discovery of the twentieth century was made in Mesopotamia, a flat plain between the Tigris and Euphrates rivers in the Middle East. This area is generally conceded to be the birthplace of civilization, the area in which the organized mode of living that we call civilized developed even earlier than it did in Egypt. While Egypt had a civilization that continued unbroken for almost four thousand years, Mesopotamia was ruled by a succession of related, yet distinct groups. Its history is more fragmented and less well known than the history of Egypt.

The great archaeological discovery in Mesopotamia was made by Sir Charles Leonard Woolley at a place called Ur, a city mentioned in the Bible as the home of the Hebrew patriarch Abraham. Long before Abraham lived, Ur was a city of the Sumerians, quite possibly the earliest civilized people in history. Woolley was excavating a Sumerian burial ground when he quite unexpectedly came upon the remains of a mass burial. Dozens of people had been interred in a chambered tomb. They had all been sacrificed in some sort of a ritual that attended the main burial, in this case the burial of a female, probably a queen. Other tombs showing that the Sumarians practiced human sacrifice were unearthed in the same region. This find came as a complete surprise, since nothing that had previously been known of the Sumarians hinted that human sacrifice was part of their culture.

The tombs, or death pits, as Woolley grimly named them, contained a number of golden objects, cups, goblets, bowls, cosmetic boxes, all of exquisite workmanship. The most elaborate piece of golden jewelry was the queen's headdress, a complex arrangement of golden leaves and flowers. One writer described it as a "veritable flower garden." The queen's female attendants, who had been sacrificed in the ceremony, wore simpler versions of their mistress's golden headdress. All of these headdresses were made from paper-thin sheets of gold. They were too fragile to have ever been worn by a living person, and were obviously made specially for the sacrifice.

The Sumerians never used the sheer mass of gold that was used by the Egyptians, probably because the area in which they lived contained no native gold. All gold had to be imported to Mesopotamia.

The people of the ancient Middle East made golden statues and images, as well as golden jewelry, but little of this material survives. In the Bible there is the story of how Moses found, to his horror, that the "Children of Israel" were worshiping the image of a calf made from golden ornaments they had melted down. That was considered a great sin, but it indicates that the practice of worshiping golden images was not uncommon.

Gold itself was not considered sinful by the Israelites. When King Solomon built his temple, gold was used profusely in the holiest place, the inner sanctuary.

> He made also all the furnishings for the house of the Lord; the golden altar and the golden table upon which was set the Bread of the Presence; the lamp-stands of red gold, five on the right side and five on the left side of the inner shrine; the flowers, lamps, and tongs, of gold; the cups, snuffers, tossing-bowls, saucers, and firepans, of red gold; and the panels for the doors of the inner sanctuary, the Most Holy Place, and for the doors of the house, of gold. (1 Kings 7:48–51)

It is recorded in the Bible that Solomon received an enormous quantity of gold from the Queen of Sheba, and from the land of Ophir. Translating biblical weights and measures into modern ones is an inexact business; the best we can estimate from the Bible is that Solomon was getting something like thirty-six thousand pounds of gold a year. That is a staggering quantity, even with today's mining and refining techniques. If we allow for considerable exaggeration, there still is good reason to believe that Solomon received a lot of gold. But where was the land of the Queen of Sheba, and where was Ophir? No one today knows.

The term, King Solomon's mines, was popularized by the British adventure writer Sir Henry Rider Haggard, who located the source of Solomon's gold in central

Africa. Haggard was a writer of fiction, but many others, with no more information than Haggard possessed, have seriously suggested dozens of other locations as the source of Solomon's gold. There are a large number of ancient gold mining sites that would have been within the reach of Solomon's trading ships. His gold could have come from any of them. The most popular current candidate for Ophir is a place called Mahd adh Dhahab in Saudi Arabia.

The golden objects of the temple have long since vanished. There is evidence that at least some of them were still intact as late as the third or fourth century A.D. They were, however, brought as spoils to Constantinople, and after that nothing more was ever heard of them.

There is no more romantic story in all archaeology than that of Heinrich Schliemann who, while still a boy, had become fascinated by the epic tales of the Greek poet Homer. Schliemann made a fortune in business and then retired young in 1871 in order to devote the rest of his life and his fortune to finding proof that the incidents in Homer's poems were true. He is widely regarded as the discoverer of Troy, a site that had eluded professionally trained archaeologists for so long that many had decided that the place didn't exist at all.

Even today professional archaeologists are not nearly as enthusiastic about Schliemann's accomplishments as is the general public. They point out that while he did find an ancient city in Turkey (actually seven of them, one atop the other), there is no assurance that any of the cities was Homer's Troy.

Schliemann's crude methods of digging are most deplored, for while finding much, he also destroyed much in his enthusiasm. Some consider him little better than a vulgar treasure hunter.

There is no doubt that the lure of gold contributed much to Schliemann's passion. And he found gold, too. While searching for Troy he noticed what he thought was a gleam of gold in the soil, and began to dig recklessly, though a tower that rose above the trench where he was working threatened to collapse on him at any moment. He was rewarded with, among other things, eighty-seven hundred gold rings, sixty gold earrings, a gold goblet, and two elaborate gold diadems, one of which consisted of 16,353 individual pieces of gold.

Schliemann immediately assumed that he had discovered the golden treasure of King Priam of Troy that was mentioned by Homer. As it turned out, these golden pieces came from a far earlier time.

After Troy, Schliemann set off to discover another place mentioned by Homer, "Golden Mycenae," the residence and burial place of King Agamemnon. Once again he was spectacularly successful. While excavating a series of shaft graves, he discovered the bodies of three men with gold weapons beside them, gold breastplates on their chests, and gold death masks covering their faces. One of these masks showed a strong, proud face with a luxuriant beard and curling mustache. It was the very image of a warlike king. Schliemann promptly announced that he had "gazed on the face of Agamemnon." Once again his romantic enthusiasm had run away with him. Like Priam's treasure, the golden mask of Agamemnon had been made in an earlier time. But there can be no quibbling over the fact that this was an extremely important find, and that the mask itself is one of the most important golden artifacts of antiquity.

Schliemann was a man with extraordinary luck, yet he just narrowly missed making yet another "golden" discovery. While digging at Mycenae, he found some artifacts that reminded him of objects found on the island of Crete. This gave him the idea that Crete, too, might have been the home of an important early civilization. He began negotiations to buy a promising archaeological site on Crete, but the asking price was too high, and he gave up the project. The discovery of the great Minoan civilization centered on Crete was left to others.

Crete has no gold of its own, so the Minoans, a sea power and a nation of traders, had to import what they used. Most of their gold probably came from Egypt. Not much gold work has been found on Crete, perhaps because most of it had been taken away and melted down after Minoan civilization collapsed. (The reason for the collapse of Minoan civilization is one of those eternally fascinating archaeological mysteries.) But it is equally possible that the Minoans never used much gold.

What they did use was crafted to perfection. From the scanty evidence we possess, it appears as though the Minoans were masterful in their use of hammered gold. One pendant on display in the museum in Herakleion on Crete is composed of a golden string from which hang twenty-five small droplets or "tears" of gold.

The Egyptians and the Minoans belonged to highly developed civilizations. That they should have produced magnificent goldwork is not altogether surprising. Yet, some of the finest gold pieces of antiquity come from a people whom we cannot really consider civilized at all. These were the Scythians, a warlike and nomadic people, from the steppes of Russia. The Scythians were contemporaries of the classical Greeks, about 600 to 800 B.C. Most of what we know about them comes from scattered references in Greek literature. They were horsemen who held sway over a large, but loose empire of the Steppes. They had no written language, built no cities, and didn't even have permanent homes. Yet, they produced golden ornaments, often in fantastic animal shapes, that are unparallelled in strangeness and beauty. An exhibition of Scythian gold held at the Metropolitan Museum in 1975 proved to be an astonishment, even to the most jaded observers of gold.

The Scythians may have placed such a high value on golden ornaments, precisely because they were a nomadic people. Since they had no permanent homes or temples, all symbols of wealth had to be portable.

Both the Greeks and the Persians are believed to have been heavy users of gold, though little of their goldwork has survived. All the classical Greek statues, which we now think of as being made from pure white marble, were originally colored, often very garishly, and important statues were overlaid with gold. The famous Greek sculptor Phidias, who lived in the fifth century B.C., was supposed to have made a thirty-five-foot-high statue of the goddess Athena of ivory, and to have covered it with two thousand pounds of removable gold sheet. His enormous statue of Zeus was also made of ivory. Clothed in robes of gold and golden sandals, it was seated on a golden throne. The amount of gold used to decorate these statues must have been tremendous.

The Etruscans, a rather mysterious people who were an important power on the Italian peninsula before the rise of Rome, were marvelous goldsmiths. They created gold filigree work and used granular decoration with a delicacy that had never been seen before, and has not been equaled since. As always, most of the gold of the Etruscans has long since been tossed back into the melting pot, no matter how great its artistic value. But, from the limited examples that survive, and from what can be learned from Etruscan paintings and sculpture, it is obvious that the Etruscans placed a high value on gold decoration.

The Romans were heavily influenced by both the Greeks and the Etruscans. Therefore, it is more than a bit surprising that they do not seem to have cared very much about golden ornaments. In its beginnings Rome had been poor, a land without gold supplies of its own. But, at its height, the Roman Empire commanded the gold supply of a major portion of the world. Still the Romans never became good goldworkers. They used gold coins and hoarded gold in the form of bars and bricks, but they never wore a great deal of gold decoration. Rings were the most common golden ornaments and a really showy Roman would wear a ring on every finger.

It is a cliché to call the Romans a practical rather than an artistic or a religious people. Yet, there is a fair measure of truth in the statement. An odd streak of puritanism ran through Roman society. The Romans had laws against wearing fancy clothing, or a great deal of jewelry. At times, citizens of Rome were limited to wearing less than one ounce of gold. Though such laws were not always enforced, they may have helped to discourage craftsmanship in the metal.

We have only touched upon gold as it was used in a limited number of ancient societies. To provide a complete picture is far beyond the scope of this book. Gold was a precious substance in ancient China, and new discoveries are revealing the high degree of skill attained by Chinese goldsmiths of the ancient dynasties.

Central and southern Africa are dotted with ancient gold mines. Unfortunately, very little of the gold jewelry and ornamentation made in black Africa survives today, but there is just enough of it to give us a hint of the great treasures that must have been melted down in the not-so-distant past.

The Incas of South America called gold "the sweat of the sun," and temples were adorned with a magnificent golden disk representing the sun. Indeed, it was the very riches of the Indian civilizations of South and Central America that, as we shall see in a later chapter, brought about their destruction at the hands of the gold-hungry conquistadors.

Goldworking began with the Egyptians, and relatively few societies since that of these ancient people have held the metal in such high regard, but no society that has ever come in prolonged contact with gold has remained indifferent to it. Our lust for gold comes down to us from the very dawn of recorded history, and before.

AVGVSTVS DIVI·F
CAESAR AVGVSTVS

3

GOLD AS MONEY

Perhaps you have heard the expression, "rich as Croesus." There really was a Croesus, and he really was rich. In the sixth century B.C., Croesus was king of Lydia, a kingdom in Asia Minor, or what is now Turkey. It was a wealthy country, and much of its wealth was in gold.

The source of Lydia's gold was the river called the Pactolus (now called the Gediz or Sarabat). All the gold has long since been taken from the river, but in ancient

POSITE: *Roman gold coins from the time of Augustus Caesar.* merican Numismatic Society)

times it was one of the greatest gold-bearing rivers the world had ever known. The gold was washed down from Mt. Tmolus, the source of the river. So famous was the river's gold that the Greeks said the legendary King Midas had transferred his ability to turn everything he touched into gold to the Pactolus.

Lydia reached the height of her wealth and power under King Gyges and his successor Croesus. Croesus has been credited for a number of things, among them the introduction of coins to the world.

Actually, Croesus didn't really introduce coins. Remember, the early Egyptian king Narimer had fourteen-gram gold bars stamped with the royal seal, which may have circulated as money, though they were probably too valuable to be used in ordinary commerce.

Throughout the Middle East a golden coin called a shekel was in use long before the time of Croesus. This coin was familiar to the Hebrews and is mentioned frequently in the Bible. The Hebrew shekel had a fairly standard weight of about 16.4 grams, but the purity of the gold in the coin was often in doubt. Much of the gold found in the Middle East is really a gold-silver alloy called electrum; pure gold was rare. It was difficult, if not impossible, for even the most honest trader to know the ratio of valuable gold to less valuable silver in each shekel, for the quality varied enormously. In such a situation the temptation to cheat would be enormous. Testing the purity of each coin was impractical. So, in an ordinary transaction, the buyer and seller would argue not only about the price of the goods, but about the value of the shekel used to pay for them. It was a highly unsatisfactory situation, and most trade was still conducted by the direct barter of goods.

It is possible that King Gyges may actually have been the first to issue gold coins in Lydia, but the credit is commonly given to Croesus, who reigned from 560 to 546 B.C. and issued two coins, one of gold and another of silver. The ratio between the two coins was standardized. Thirteen and one-third silver coins were worth one gold coin.

Croesus's coins were crudely shaped oblongs, stamped with his royal emblem: the heads of a lion and a bull facing each other. The coins weren't beautiful, but they were reliable and comparatively plentiful. The stamp meant that the power and wealth of the king of Lydia guaranteed the purity of their contents. Since trustworthy coins had never been known before, those of Croesus became enormously popular and were widely distributed throughout the Mediterranean world.

Why was this particular development so important? Ray Vicker, a staff member of the *Wall Street Journal*, has written in his book, *The Realms of Gold:*

> It is difficult to overestimate the importance of this development, for man now had a medium of exchange which had eluded him for thousands of years. A voyage to distant lands could be made by a ship captain with only a bag of coins as his cargo and he could return with a shipload of merchandise. A producer with a surplus of goods could sell that surplus for gold or silver coins, and these coins would serve as a store of value long after the merchandise might have deteriorated had it been kept.

Croesus—in addition to his riches and the introduction of standardized coins—was also famous for his devotion to the Oracle at Delphi. The Oracle was a shrine in Greece where, upon the payment of a fee, the priestess of the shrine would answer questions about the future. The answers were generally more ambiguous than useful, but this didn't shake Croesus's faith one bit. He sent the shrine hundreds of ingots of gold and electrum, and dedicated a golden life-sized statue of a woman to Delphi. He also presented the shrine with a golden bowl that weighed 875 pounds and a 1,000-pound golden lion. All in all, it is said that Croesus deposited at least 7,500 pounds of gold at Delphi. And for that price he expected answers.

Around the year 540 B.C. Lydia was menaced by the Persian Empire, which was rapidly expanding under the leadership of its brilliant founder Cyrus the Great. Croesus was unsure as to whether to wait for the Persians to come to him, or to go on the offensive and attack them. Naturally he turned to Delphi. Croesus was told that if he attacked the Persians, a great empire would be destroyed.

Croesus, who wanted to attack anyway, assumed that the Oracle had predicted the destruction of the Persian Empire. He mounted an attack against the Persians, was defeated, and lost his lands to the victors. The king of the Lydians was more than a little annoyed at the Oracle. He sent off an angry message demanding to know why, after all the gifts he had showered upon Delphi, the Oracle had given him the wrong answer. The Oracle's reply was, "You didn't ask which empire."

Since that time the term, Delphic reply, has been applied to any ambiguous or obscure answer.

Another story told of Croseus is that Cyrus was so impressed by his wisdom that he quite literally plucked him from the flames that were to be his funeral pyre, and took him back to Persia as an adviser.

How much truth there is in these stories about Croesus is difficult to determine. But we do know that the Persians adopted the Lydian bimetallic coin system. At its height, under Darius I, Cyrus's successor, the Persian Empire was enormous. It stretched all the way from Greece to India, and contained not only the gold-rich land of Lydia, but the far greater golden riches of Egypt. The Persian gold *daric* and silver *siglos* became the standard currency for this huge region.

Darius had his own portrait stamped on the coins, thus giving what amounted to a personal assurance of the purity of the metals that they contained. This began the custom of monarchs putting their own faces on coins, and later, on paper money, a custom that continues to this day. The U.S. mint uses only the likenesses of dead presidents; in Britain, however, it is still the reigning monarch whose likeness appears on the currency.

As time went on the symbols stamped on coins became less a guarantee of the metallic purity of the coin, and more of a piece of political propaganda or statement of political aims. New rulers would immediately begin issuing coins stamped with their own likenesses, or with symbols that were important to them. It was a way of attempting to legitimize any transfer of power.

This habit has aided historians immensely. There is even a special area of study called numismatics, the study of money. Whereas records of many ancient societies are either scanty or entirely absent, most of them issued currency of one sort or another. The coins, particularly if they are gold, withstand the ravages of time far better than any written records. Coins can help to establish the dates of particular sites. If the coin of one nation is found at a place far distant from its origin, this indicates trade, or perhaps conquest.

The inscriptions or symbols on coins may even have a good deal to say about the chief concerns of a particular society. For example, when the Roman general Mark Antony ruled Egypt he issued silver *denarii* with his own portrait on them. But these coins also contained an inscription that hailed Cleopatra, the Egyptian queen and his mistress as "Queen of Kings and of her Sons that are Kings." That was a clear indication that Antony intended to have his sons, by Cleopatra, rule Egypt. At Rome, Antony pursued a different policy. He issued a gold coin with his portrait on one side, and a picture of his son Antyllus, by his Roman wife, on the other. This was an indication that as far as Rome was concerned Antony's heir was to be Roman. His coinage clearly shows that Antony was hedging his bets.

While the Persians adopted Croesus's coins, they did not make any innovations in the system. Indeed, they were very conservative in their use of gold and silver coins. It was Persian policy to keep most of their supply of precious metals in reserve in the form of bars, or turn it into objects of art and jewelry. The Persians, however, were lavish in their use of "gold diplomacy." They never went into a battle unnecessarily, preferring to buy out their enemies rather than fight them. The Greeks, who were kept effectively divided by Persian gold, had a word for the purchase of friendship. It was *Medizing*, for the Persians were closely related to the Medes, and the words Persians and Medes were often linked or used interchangeably.

One enemy that the Persians could not buy, though they certainly tried hard enough, was the Macedonian conqueror, Alexander the Great. In a military career that lasted less than ten years, Alexander not only brought down the great Persian Empire, but every other state that stood in his path. At its height Alexander's empire extended all the way from Greece to what is now the southern part of the Soviet Union and the northern part of India. It was an explosion of conquest unmatched in human history.

In the process of conquest, Alexander made much of the known world's gold supply his own personal property. Unlike the Persians, who had been conservative in the minting of coins, Alexander had a large percentage of his vast treasure minted as coins. These he distributed freely to his friends, and to his ever-growing army.

Alexander's army was constantly on the move, and in order to keep from lugging large quantities of gold coins around, caches of coins were sometimes buried, to be picked up later. But occasionally these caches were not picked up, and from time to time throughout history bits of this buried treasure from Alexander's army have turned up. The last major find was made in Turkey in 1850, when workmen uncovered two copper pots filled with gold *staters*. Some two thousand coins were finally rounded up by the Turkish government but the horde must have been far larger. Most of the coins quickly disappeared into the pockets of the workmen who found them.

In Alexander's day there was hardly anything that might be called a world gold market. Yet, the conqueror's sudden release of vast quantities of gold that had once been locked up in the Persian treasury created what may well have been the world's first monetary inflation.

By the time Alexander's army had reached the Punjab region of India, it had been at war and on the move almost constantly for nearly nine years. They had conquered much of the known world, and despite Alexander's wishes to conquer the rest of it, the soldiers would go no farther. The disappointed conqueror turned back, but died before reaching home. He was thirty-two years old.

The empire that had been won so rapidly broke up even more rapidly. But while his empire did not last, Alexander's conquests did produce permanent changes in the history of the Western world. Not the least of these changes was that the *staters* and *drachmas* that had made up Alexander's currency became the first true world-wide currency. The coins were recognized and accepted from the Nile to the Indus and from the Black Sea to the Indian Ocean. Because they were reliable and plentiful, they stimulated and facilitated world trade.

Early in history the center of gold production was Egypt. Later it shifted to Asia Minor and in the world after Alexander's conquests the center had shifted once again, to Spain. Spain was at that time under the control of Carthage, a city in North Africa. Carthage was originally set up as a colony of the seafaring Phoenicians, but it had long been a wealthy, powerful, and independent city. The ships of Carthage probably roamed farther than any earlier ships. Every few years someone comes up with what purports to be a new piece of evidence that proves that the Carthagenians discovered America a century or two before the start of the Christian era. While this is not altogether impossible, for the ships of Carthage did go a long way out into the Atlantic Ocean, so far the evidence has been less than satisfactory.

Carthage is not one of the best known of ancient societies. If it is known for anything at all, it is for its long and bitter struggle with Rome. This struggle, fought between 264 and 146 B.C. and called the Punic Wars, ended in the defeat and destruction of Carthage, and the first major world victory of the rising Romans.

So Carthage has come down to us with a reputation as a loser, which really isn't fair. The wonder is not that Carthage lost to Rome, but that it had been able to compete so long, and so successfully. Rome had a comparatively large population, and a well-trained citizen army to depend upon. The Romans could call out troops from their allies throughout Italy. Carthage had a tiny population and no friendly hinterland from which to draw aid. The Carthagenian army was made up almost entirely of mercenaries. The use of mercenary troops was extremely common in the ancient world (and is becoming more common in the modern world, though often we fail to acknowledge this fact). Mercenaries can fight well, if they are well led, well armed, and well paid, especially the latter. The Carthagenian mercenaries were paid largely in gold from the mines of Spain. One of Rome's major concerns throughout the Punic Wars was to separate Carthage from the source of her gold.

Arnold Herman Ludwig Heeren, a German historian, wrote: "Rome trusted to itself and its sword, Carthage to its gold and its mercenaries. The greatness of Rome was founded upon a rock, that of Carthage upon sand and gold dust."

But Rome did not scorn the gold dust of Carthage. The victorious Romans took over the Spanish mines and worked them as hard as the Carthagenians ever had. It is estimated that by the early years of the Christian era the mines of Spain were producing as much as twenty thousand pounds of gold every year.

We have already commented on the rather disappointing quality of the gold craftsmanship of the Romans. But Romans were certainly not immune to the lure of gold, or blind to the political advantages that gold could bring. The devotion of Rome's citizen army was one of those qualities that allowed it to conquer a great empire. But, as Rome's territory expanded, there simply weren't enough citizens to fill the growing needs of the army. Besides, Rome's increasing prosperity made the trade of soldiering less and less attractive to Rome's citizens. So Rome began doing what Carthage and many other societies had done before: She began to hire mercenaries.

The army became the most powerful force in the Roman Empire. Without the loyalty of the army, an emperor might quickly find himself deprived of his throne and his life. The best way of maintaining the loyalty of the army was with gold. Every time an emperor's position became shaky, his first move was to raise the pay of the army, so that they would not become restless and begin looking around for a new leader. Sometimes this ploy worked, sometimes it didn't.

The policy of courting the favor of the army at all costs reached its height in the year 191 A.D. when, for a brief period, the entire Roman Empire was actually for sale to the highest bidder. The emperor Commodus, an eccentric and unstable fellow, had just been murdered. As his successor, the Praetorian Guard (the elite troops that guarded the city of Rome and the person of the emperor) chose a general called Pertinax. But Pertinax was unable to supply the army with several bonuses they had been promised. In addition, he turned out to be a stern disciplinarian, so he too was quickly murdered.

There were now two candidates for the succession, Sulpicianus and Julianus. The Praetorian Guard decided to sell the throne to whichever of the two offered them a higher sum, and so a mock auction was held. The Roman historian Dio Cassius did not hide his disgust at this sordid event:

> There ensued a most disgraceful business and one unworthy of Rome. For, just as if it had been in some market or auction-room, the city and its entire empire were auctioned off. The sellers were the ones who had slain their emperor, and the would-be buyers were Sulpicianus and Julianus, who vied to outbid each other, one from inside the camp and the other from outside. They gradually raised their bids up to five thousand *denarii* per soldier. Some of the soldiers would carry word to Julianus "Sulpicianus offers so much; how much more do you make it?" and to Sulpicianus in turn, "Julianus promises so much; how much do you raise him?"

Julianus finally won by offering over six thousand *denarii* per soldier. His reign, however, lasted only sixty-six days, for he was overthrown by Septimius Severus, a general of one of the provincial armies. The Praetorians were bested by Severus's troops, who then proclaimed him emperor. Severus was a first-rate ruler but his power rested entirely on the army, and he and every emperor after him had to continue to supply the army with as much gold as they could possibly muster.

The Romans were also adept at using gold for political and military purposes. They were forced to rely increasingly on gold to buy off the barbarian hordes that were threatening the borders of the empire.

The practice of buying off barbarians with gold continued, and indeed increased after Christianity became the official religion of the Roman Empire. In the year 452, Attila the Hun was ravaging the lands of the Roman Empire. His armies were at the very gates of Rome, and the city did not possess a military force remotely capable of stopping him. But, before the city was actually entered, there was a dramatic meeting between Pope Leo I and the Hun leader. As a result the Huns turned back, and the following year Attila died and his empire broke up. Christians hailed Attila's dramatic turnabout as a miracle, brought about by the direct intervention of God. But the miracle was aided considerably by the transfer of vast quantities of gold from the Romans to the Huns. The city of Rome itself was of no interest or use to the Huns.

As a matter of policy, friendly barbarian leaders were given a variety of honors and titles that were commemorated with the presentation of a valuable golden medallion. This was a polite fiction that made a bribe look slightly less like a bribe.

Though the Romans controlled the gold resources of much of the world, their need for gold rapidly outstripped their resources. The emperors rarely had enough money to satisfy their grandiose ambitions. To close the gap they began debasing the coins. That is, they put less precious metal, gold or silver into the coins, which had once been pure or nearly pure gold and silver. The coins were supposed to retain the same value, but the Romans never really accepted this idea. To them the coin that had less precious metal in it was worth less, and emperors were required to debase the coinage still further in order to stay even. The gold or silver itself did not go down in value, there was just less of it in the coins.

The process worked this way: Let us say the soldiers had received a bonus of five hundred *denarii* each. The *denarius* was the standard silver coin. The standard gold coin was the *aureus,* which was worth twenty-five *denarii.* But, the *denarius* and the *aureus* had been debased since the last time. Each now contained one-third less precious metal than it had before. Thus, in order to simply stay even, soldiers would expect a bonus of 666 *denarii,* and if the empire was in a shaky position, heavily dependent upon the loyalty of the soldiers as it usually was, they could demand considerably more.

The result of this process was inflation, a term with which we are all familiar today. Since Roman coins were standard throughout much of the world, the inflation was world-wide. People lost confidence in Roman coins, and at various periods this created severe economic problems and hardships.

In addition to gold and silver coins, the Romans also used coins of bronze, and then of brass and copper. These coins were strictly tokens; that is, the metal itself was not worth the value assigned to the coin. These coins were small change, and the Romans generally accepted them for their convenience. But they could never accept the token principle for gold and silver coins. Thus, when less gold was put in a coin the Romans valued it at a lower rate, no matter what the emperor and his treasurers might say.

Just how important the debasement of the coinage was in contributing to the decline and ultimate fall of the Roman Empire is a matter of some dispute among historians. George Finlay, an English historian, thought that it was important indeed:

> In reviewing the causes which contributed to the decline of the wealth and the dimunition of the Roman Empire, it is necessary to take into account the depreciation of the coinage, which frequently robbed large classes of the industrious citizens of a great part of their wealth, reduced the value of property, produced confusion in legal contracts, and anarchy in prices in the public markets. The evils which have resulted from the enormous depreciation of the Roman coinage at several periods can only be understood by a chronological record of the principal changes, and by remembering that each issue of a depreciated coinage was an act of bankruptcy on the part of a reigning emperor.

Other historians, while not denying the problems associated with debased coinage, doubt if it had such cataclysmic effects. They attribute the decline of Rome to a host of factors, of which debasement of the coinage was one, but only one and a minor one at that. They see debasement as more of a symptom than a cause.

The problem is never going to be settled. We have enough trouble trying to understand the economic situation in the modern world. It is hopeless to think that we can ever truly understand the economy of any ancient society, about which reliable information is either scanty, or missing entirely. But the argument will go on, anyway. The argument really concerns more than Rome, or any other ancient society. It is an argument between two distinct points of view on economics, indeed about society as a whole. The two camps might be called the "chrysophyles" (*chryso* is the Greek word for gold) and the "chrysophobes," the gold lovers and the gold haters.

The chrysophyles attach enormous importance to gold. They believe that a sound currency, backed by gold, if not actually made out of gold, is the very core of a nation's economic health. The chysophobes think that gold is overrated, and that the economic health of a country should not be tied exclusively to the amount of gold the country happens to have stored in its vaults. Indeed, they believe that in the modern world, gold is superfluous. There are a variety of intermediate positions between these two extremes, and the points of view will be discussed in greater detail later on. But it is important at this stage to know that such positions exist, and that they heavily influence even what historians say about the past.

If the chrysophyles had to pick an ideal society, it

might well be Byzantium. In 325 A.D. the Roman Emperor Constantine surveyed the wreckage of Rome itself, and decided to move his capital eastward to the Bosporus. He established his new capital at a little town called Byzantium. Constantine rebuilt it into a magnificent city, which he named after himself, Constantinople. The old name ultimately reasserted itself. For a while the whole Roman Empire was ruled from Constantinople, but finally it broke into two distinct parts, eastern and western. The eastern half, called Byzantium, was ruled from Constantinople and continued to exist long after the western half of the old empire, ruled from Rome, had dissolved.

When Constantine changed capitals he also reformed the currency. He created a new gold piece, the *solidus* or *bezant.* It contained sixty-five grains of gold, and became the key currency of the Byzantine Empire, and indeed of the entire world. The gold *solidus* was accepted from China to Africa. The coin retained its full value for nearly eight hundred years, a record unmatched in human history.

By the twelfth century, however, Byzantine power was in severe decline. The once glorious empire had been reduced practically to the city of Constantinople alone, and the Turks were sharpening their scimitars for the final kill. The kill was long delayed and the city, to practically everyone's astonishment, did manage to hold on until 1435. By that time, however, its days of golden glory were long long past.

The twelfth-century debasement of the *solidus* was brought about by adding 25 percent more base metals to the gold in the coin. Further debasements followed.

Extreme chrysophyles see the fall of Byzantium as resulting directly from this watering-down of its currency. That position, however, is hard to support, for the very survival of Byzantium was entirely improbable. It was a Christian city, in the midst of a Moslem world, and faced with the vigorous and expanding Turkish Empire. Even a full-value *solidus* could not overcome all of that.

But while Byzantium lasted gold played an extraordinarily large part in its life. Fairly early in their history the Byzantines learned that they could not rely heavily on military power. Byzantium became a commercial empire that drew its wealth more from trade than conquest, though the Byzantine navy was effective in defense of the city itself. Mainly, enemies were to be bought off or simply awed into submission.

A favorite tactic of the Byzantines was to invite potential enemies to the city, show them the golden splendors of the palaces and churches, and finally introduce them to the emperor himself. The emperor, wearing a golden crown, golden slippers, and a robe woven from golden thread, appeared more of a golden image, than a living person. That is how he was meant to appear. And the trick worked, for far longer than anyone had a right to expect that it would.

4

THE ALCHEMISTS' GOLD

And then, following my book word for word, I made projection of the Red Stone upon half a pound of mecury, in the presence of Pernelle only, in the same house, the five-and-twentieth day of April following, the same year [1382], about five o'clock in the evening; which I transmuted truly into about the same quantity of pure gold, most

OPPOSITE: *Alchemists at work.*

> certainly better than ordinary gold, being more soft and pliable . . . Pernelle understood it as well as I, because she helped me in my operations, and without doubt if she had undertaken to do it herself she would have attained to the end and perfection thereof. I had indeed enough when I had once done it, but I found exceeding great pleasure and delight in seeing and contemplating the admirable works of Nature.

So wrote Nicolas Flamel, a fourteenth-century Parisian alchemist, and one of those most widely credited with accomplishing "the Great Work" of transforming base metals into gold.

Alchemy was both a process and a philosophy. Its practitoners believed they would be able to understand and control nature. Alchemist Flamel said he found the secret of the process in an ancient Hebrew book that had fallen into his hands by chance. Even so, he had to travel throughout Europe to find someone who could help him translate and understand the obscure work. It took years of labor in his own laboratory for Flamel to perfect the processes that he had learned from the volume. Flamel is said to have performed the transmutation only five times in his life. He never sought great wealth, though he lived an exceedingly comfortable life, and upon his death left a substantial sum to a variety of religious and charitable institutions.

There is, of course, not a scrap of credible evidence that Flamel, or anyone else, ever transmuted base metals into gold. Flamel's only witness was Pernelle, his wife. The book from which he allegedly obtained the great secret has never been found. His modest wealth could have been accumulated by perfectly ordinary means; his wife had been well off, and before plunging into alchemy, Flamel had been a successful copyist.

While the transmutation of base metals into gold is theoretically possible, the cost of such an operation would far, far exceed the value of the gold produced. Besides, the transmutation would only be possible on the nuclear level. It would have been quite impossible by the methods and equipment available to Flamel or other alchemists.

At first glance, alchemy appears to be one of mankind's maddest quests. For centuries men (and a few women) pursued a goal that we now know to be unreachable. Yet, more often than not, the alchemists were the most educated and enlightened members of the community in which they lived.

Alchemy was no leisure-time hobby, either. It involved years of tedious experimentation, endless hours spent bent over furnaces and crucibles, breathing foul and often health-destroying fumes. When not actually in the laboratory, the alchemist was engaged in reading, or trying to read, the unfathomable works of other alchemists.

Alchemy did not produce great wealth; indeed, it was expensive. Flamel, who died well off, was an exception. The famous alchemist, Paracelsus, who was also rumored to have mastered the transmutation of base metals into gold, died a drunken pauper. And many alchemists would have envied even that fate. A passion for expensive alchemical experiments ruined more than one great fortune.

Alchemy was dangerous in another way. Orthodox

church officials looked upon the pursuit as suspiciously close to heresy or sorcery; either could be an offense punishable at the stake. Sometimes alchemists were honored figures at the courts of the nobility. More often they were ignored, persecuted, and occasionally executed.

And yet, to look upon alchemy as just another example of human foolishness isn't at all fair. The alchemists didn't know what we now know, that it is impossible to change base metals into gold by a combination of ordinary heating, cooling, and adding other materials. Within the limits of the alchemists' view of the world, such a transformation appeared entirely possible, if only one got the procedure exactly right. There were always the intriguing tales relating how other alchemists, like Flamel, had done it. Two centuries after Flamel's death, people were still picking over the property he had owned in an effort to find the secret they passionately believed was hidden there.

Then, there was the lure of gold itself. To the alchemist, and indeed to many others, gold was more than just a valuable metal; it was a symbol of everything that was good, fine, and pure in the world. There is, in fact, both a chemical and a spiritual side to alchemy. The transformation of a "common and base" metal such as lead to the "pure and noble" metal, gold, was likened to the transformation of a base, gross, and material soul to one of great spiritual purity. According to some alchemists, only the individual who had spiritually transformed himself would be able to perform the transmutation of base metal to gold. Sometimes it is difficult to tell whether the alchemist is writing of a material or a spiritual transformation, or both.

The idea of perfection that alchemists attached to gold is well expressed in a thirteenth-century work called *The Mirror of Alchemy,* which is attributed to the English philosopher and scientist Roger Bacon: "I must tell you that Nature always intends and strives to the perfection of Gold; but many accidents, coming between, change the metals."

In addition to the gold itself, there was "the philosophers stone," an incredible material that when applied to any base metal would turn it to gold. The stone could also be made into a liquid that conferred immortality upon those who drank it. At least some alchemists appeared to believe that.

In all honesty, we must admit that we will probably never really be able to penetrate all the processes and theories of alchemy. While we have a huge number of surviving alchemical works, they are all extremely difficult to understand. In large measure, the obscurity was deliberate; the alchemists wanted to keep their secrets. If one alchemist discovered the key to "the Great Work," he didn't want that secret stolen from him. Also, since alchemy embraced so many dangerously unorthodox ideas, alchemists found it necessary to cloak their procedures in obscure phrases.

Alchemists also insisted that secrecy was necessary in order to keep the great powers they possessed out of the hands of the greedy and unworthy. Thomas Norton, a fifteenth-century English alchemist, warned in a poem entitled "The Ordinal of Alchemy":

> "This art must ever secret be,
> The cause whereof is this, as ye may see;

If one evil man had thereof all his will,
All Christian peace he might easily spill,
And with his pride he might pull down
Rightful kings and princes of renown."

Finally, there were a large number of plain fakers in the ranks of alchemists. They hid their fraud under a cloud of high-sounding but utterly meaningless phrases.

The symbolism used in alchemical writing, though always difficult, was often quite beautiful. One is likely to run across passages like the following:

> But when we marry the crowned king with the red daughter, she will conceive a son in the gentle fire, and shall nourish him through our fire . . . Then is he transformed, and his tincture remains red as flesh. Our son of royal birth takes his tincture from the fire, and death, darkness and the waters flee away. The dragon shuns the light of the sun, and our dead son shall live. The king comes forth from the fire and rejoices in the marriage.

Apparently, a chemical process is being described here, but which one? It is impossible to know for certain, because the symbolism employed by the alchemists was not consistent.

The alchemists also illustrated their works with a variety of strangely symbolic drawings. Alchemical books were filled with dragons, snakes, kings, queens, and phoenixes rising from the ashes, and scenes of dismemberment and cannibalism. But, like the words of the alchemist, his drawings are also often impossible to interpret.

As far as we can determine, what we call alchemy began in ancient Egypt, though there was a similar development in China. Chinese alchemy was most concerned with making a potion for immortality. But the Chinese alchemists did try from time to time to make gold, though they were forbidden to do so by imperial edict. Whether there was any connection between Chinese and Western alchemy is unknown at present.

As we have already seen, the Egyptians were extremely skilled in working with gold. They had also reached a high level of skill in producing silver and copper alloys that looked a great deal like gold. If a substance looked like gold, the early alchemists must have reasoned, then it must really be gold, or at least on its way to becoming gold. So it appears that alchemy began with the production of gold substitutes and gold look-alikes.

Alexander the Great conquered Egypt in the fourth century B.C. and established his capital at Alexandria. After the conqueror's death Egypt was ruled from Alexandria by one of Alexander's generals, Ptolemy, and his descendants. The last of these was the celebrated Cleopatra whose kingdom was finally annexed by the Romans. For several centuries under the Ptolemies and the Romans, Alexandria was the intellectual capital of the Western world. It was a place where the cultures of Africa, Asia, and Europe mingled, as nowhere else on earth. It was the center for a whole variety of activities, and not the least of these was alchemy.

To the practical observations of the ancient Egyptian metalworkers was added a large dose of Greek philosophical speculation, and magical and mystical doctrines from many parts of the world. A large percentage of the alchemical books that were written in Alexandria during the first few centuries of the Christian era were attributed to Hermes Trismegistus. Hermes is the name of a Greek god and Trismegistus means "thrice great." So, roughly translated, the name means "three times as good as Hermes." Hermes Trismegistus was supposed to have been an Egyptian sage or god (the legends are not consistent) who lived in some incredibly ancient time. It is doubtful if there ever was any single historical character who served as a basis for the Hermes Trismegistus legends, and we are quite certain that the works attributed to him were composed by a variety of people at a much later date.

Yet, the belief in a real Hermes Trismegistus who had discovered, among other things, the process by which base metals could be changed into gold was both powerful and persistent. A whole flock of Hermetic cults flourished during Roman times. Hermetic magic and Hermetic philosophy were widely studied throughout the Middle Ages (though for the most part the Church heartily disapproved of both). Hermes Trismegistus was credited with being the father of alchemy. Even today the name persists: When something is completely sealed, we say it is hermetically sealed.

Alexandria remained the center for alchemical study and theory for centuries, though alchemy was practiced throughout first the Greek and then the Roman world. As the Roman Empire began to dissolve and barbarians took over Western Europe, interest in all learning, including alchemy, faded. While the barbarians were happy enough to take gold when they could find it, they were neither literate enough nor patient enough to read the abstruse works of the alchemists, or perform the tedious experiments. Some knowledge of alchemy remained alive in Byzantium, formerly the eastern half of the Roman Empire, but the exchange of information between Byzantium and the West was fairly limited. Alexandria was still the capital of the alchemical world. Then, in the seventh century, Alexandria and all of Egypt passed into the hands of the Muslims and they adopted alchemy with relish.

According to tradition, the first alchemist in the Muslim world was Khalid Ibn Yazid, a royal prince who lived in Damascus about 660–704. At first Khalid surrounded himself with a host of alchemical fakers, who invariably failed to make gold as they had promised. A Christian alchemist from Alexandria named Marianos heard of the prince's interest, and decided to pay him a visit in the hope of converting him from Islam to Christianity. Marianos, so the story goes, successfully made gold for Khalid. The prince's first reaction was to order that all the false alchemists be executed on the spot. This so terrified Marianos that he fled in the confusion.

A few years later one of Khalid's servants tracked down Marianos, who was then living as an obscure hermit. They persuaded (or forced) him to go back to Damascus where he revealed the secrets of alchemy to Khalid. What happened to Marianos after that is not recorded.

How much of this particular story is factual we do not know, but in later centuries a huge number of Islamic alchemical works were attributed to Prince Khalid.

The practice of alchemy remained part of the intellectual life in the Muslim world for centuries. Indeed, it may still be practiced today. In 1957 John Holmyard, a British scholar with a great interest in the history of alchemy wrote of his friend Al-Hajj Abdul-Muhyi Arab, who had died just a few years earlier:

> Abdul-Muhyi was a well-educated man, knew the Koran by heart, and had been lecturer on Koranic exegesis at the University of Lahore. As Mufti of the Shah Jehan Mosque at Woking, he spent practically the whole of his salary on conducting alchemical experiments on a portable blacksmith's forge, but, alas, without success. One of his last acts was to write a letter of introduction to an alchemist friend at Fez, the outcome of which was to give [me] the privilege of being taken to see a subterranean alchemical laboratory in the old part of that city.

The Crusades brought Western Europe into direct, if violent, contact with the world of Islam. Wars are not the best mediums for the transmission of knowledge, but as European contact with the Muslim world inevitably increased, Europeans began to realize that the Muslims were not merely a band of Satanic savages, but rather that they possessed a high culture. So it was through Arabic sources that much of the early alchemical work reached Europe. In addition, Europe received the benefit of the works of many of the pioneer alchemists of Islam.

After alchemy took root in Europe, it flourished for centuries. As we already mentioned, alchemy had a strong spiritual and mystical side. Many alchemists made significant chemical discoveries in their laboratories, and alchemy is generally regarded as the precursor of chemistry. But we are interested in gold, and in the alchemists' reported ability to be able to produce it through their arts.

As mentioned before, Nicolas Flamel was one of the most fortunate of alchemists; though he was reported to possess the secret, he lived happily and died quietly from natural causes. Not all alchemists were so lucky. Consider, for example, the short, though spectacular, career of Alexander Seton. Seton was a Scottish alchemist who appeared on the European continent in 1602. In Holland he stayed at the house of some friends, in a small town near Amsterdam. To reward his friends for the many kindnesses they had shown him Seton presented them with a little souvenir. It was a piece of gold that he had prepared from lead, in the presence of his Dutch friends.

He traveled from city to city, converting skeptics to believers in alchemy by performing transmutations before their very eyes. The testimony of numerous witnesses to Seton's prowess in producing gold are still extant.

When Seton arrived at the city of Strasbourg, he stayed at the house of a goldsmith named Gustenhover. As Seton was about to leave, he gave his host a quantity of red powder, and showed him how to make gold with the powder. Gustenhover began showing off to his friends, and soon there was a rumor that the goldsmith himself had discovered the alchemists' secret for making gold.

At that time, Rudolf II was the emperor and he was a

man utterly obsessed with the alchemical quest for gold. Rudolf had entertained and financed scores of alchemists, and when he hard of Gustenhover, he summoned the goldsmith to his court. But, by the time he received the emperor's summons, Gustenhover had used up his supply of red powder, and lacked the power to make any more. He knew that the emperor would never believe him so he tried to run away. He was captured and ended his days a prisoner in a cell in the White Tower of Rudolf's fortress.

One might suspect that Gustenhover's fate, and that of many, many other alchemists, might have made Seton cautious, but the exact reverse seems to have been true. It has often been suggested that Alexander Seton was something of an evangelist for alchemy. His habit of moving from place to place and never staying long in one town earned him the title of the Cosmopolite, and he seems to have used assumed names from time to time during his travels.

In August, 1603, Seton appeared in Cologne, a city that was overrun with failed alchemists. These unsuccessful alchemists, or puffers, as they were often called, had given the practice of alchemy a very bad name in Cologne. Seton heard a number of people, including his own host, ridicule alchemy and that enraged him. He determined to turn the ridicule back upon the scoffers. He performed several spectacular transmutations before the most voluble of the skeptics. These demonstrations were completely successful, but one of the new converts to the alchemical cause warned Seton that some prince might try to imprison him until he revealed his secret.

pleased and gave Sendivogius the title of Counsellor to his Majesty.

The rest of Sendivogius's life was quite eventful, filled with great acclaim, danger, and narrow escapes from greedy rulers, who suspected that he did in fact possess the alchemical secret. Rudolf's protection saved him from ending his days in prison or on the rack. But Rudolf, whose own grip on sanity had never been too firm, grew progressively madder. He virtually gave up effective rule and locked himself in his laboratory to putter over unsuccessful experiments.

Sendivogius was on his own again, and when he exhausted the last of Seton's powder, he was reduced to selling miracle cures and performing vulgar tricks like any other common charlatan. He died in great poverty at the age of eighty.

Alchemists continued their search for the philosopher's stone, and the bolder among them made claims that they had actually accomplished the transmutation from base metals into gold. But fewer and fewer people took the claim seriously. The last major scientific investigation of alchemical claims took place in England in 1784. James Price, a chemist and member of the prestigious scientific organization, the Royal Society, claimed that he was able to transmute mercury into either gold or silver. He successfully demonstrated the feat before a panel of distinguished men, and they were duly impressed. But none of these witnesses had any scientific training.

Needless to say, Price's claims caused a sensation. The Royal Society decided to settle the matter once and for all. They said that he should repeat his experiments with some officially appointed Fellows of the Society as witnesses. They would not easily be fooled by conjurer's tricks.

Price tried to evade the test, but extreme pressure from his friends and colleagues made this impossible. Early in August, 1784, three delegates of the society arrived at Price's laboratory. Politely excusing himself for a moment, Price drank a concoction containing prussic acid and died before the eyes of the three who had come to witness a very different demonstration.

At an inquest into Price's death, the jury decided that he had been mad, and that verdict rings true. In the past, many honest but incompetent alchemists had duped themselves into thinking that they had made gold. But Price was a good chemist, and most certainly knew what he was doing. Still, it is hard to imagine how he believed that he could get away with it for very long. He must have worked himself into a corner from which there was no escape except disgrace or death. He chose the latter.

While the popularity of alchemy has declined drastically, it has not altogether disappeared even in the West. A British alchemist named Archibald Cockrin who died in the 1960s claimed that he had made a crystal of gold grow like a plant; and there was at least one frankly alchemical society operating in London in the late 1960s.

For centuries there has been a close bond between alchemy and what we now call occultism. In 1916 H. Spencer Lewis, founder of the popular American mail-order Rosicrucian society, the Ancient Mystical Order of Rosae Crucis (AMORC), claimed that he had transmuted a piece of zinc into gold. But, according to Lewis, he had not used the traditional apparatus of the alchemist; he had, he said, used "a little known power of the mind."

But, despite occasional oddities like the claims of Lewis and Cockrin, it is abundantly clear that alchemy's day is done and we must look elsewhere for our gold.

5

EL DORADO AND OTHER GOLDEN FANTASIES

Christopher Columbus did not set sail in 1492 to prove that the world was round. Most knowledgeable mariners of the late fifteenth century assumed that it was, and had for a long time.

Nor did he set out to deliberately discover the New World. He hadn't the faintest notion that there were two large continents out in the middle of the ocean, and he was quite surprised, indeed shocked, when he ran into them.

Columbus was out to find a way to Asia that would avoid the tortuous overland route across the continent,

POSITE: *Gold mask from ancient Peru.* (Courtesy of the American useum of Natural History.)

or the tedious and often dangerous sailing around the stormy tip of Africa.

Why did Columbus undertake this long, costly, and hazardous voyage to reach Asia? The most common explanation is that he wanted to open up a trade route for the spices of the East. That may be so, but others have suggested that he was after gold as well.

Baron Alexander von Humboldt, the great nineteenth-century explorer and naturalist, contended: "America was discovered not as has been so long falsely pretended because Columbus predicted another continent, but because he sought by the west a nearer way to the gold mines of Japan and the spice countries of southeast Asia."

Columbus was certainly aware of the value of gold for he wrote, "Whoever possesses gold obtains what he will in this world, nay even by the payment of masses brings many souls into paradise." It was his failure to locate gold in the land that he had discovered that was behind Columbus's ultimate disgrace and imprisonment. Had his voyages resulted in gold for Spain, he would have remained a hero.

While Columbus didn't find any gold, Herman Cortes did. In 1519 Cortes and a small expeditionary force landed in Mexico, and within two years he had conquered the mighty Aztec Empire. Cortes didn't find gold as a prospector might; he found people who had gold, and then took what they had. As a result, while Columbus had once been brought back to Spain in chains and died almost a forgotten man, Cortes was made a marquis and died rich, though even he was a disappointed man in the end.

Francisco Pizarro started lower, and rose higher than

either Columbus or Cortes. He also found more gold, though by any reckoning he was the most undeserving of the three.

Pizarro started life as a swineherd, a task at which he was none too successful. He never learned to read, but in his wanderings he had learned to fight. Like many another poor Spaniard of the early sixteenth century, Pizarro decided to try his luck in the newly discovered lands of South America. The gold sent back by Cortes from Mexico had set many Spaniards, including Pizarro, to dreaming. And there were rumors of far more fabulous treasures in an inland kingdom called Peru.

It took years before Pizarro was able to get together the money to launch an expedition of his own to find Peru, and when he finally did, it wasn't much of an expedition. In 1532 Francisco Pizarro with 106 foot soldiers, 62 horsemen, 20 crossbows, three muskets, and a few cannons set off into the mountains of Peru to find what they hoped would be a golden kingdom. Within a year, this tiny expedition had brought down the great empire of the Inca, the mightiest empire in South America. It was an empire that built fortresses rivaling anything in Europe at that time, and roads that were superior even to those of the Romans. It was an empire that stretched three thousand miles, and could command the services of hundreds of thousands of superb warriors and the tribute of millions. It was also an empire that had piled up a vast store of gold, much of it beautifully fashioned into statuettes and jewelry of unsurpassed beauty. Yet, it was all swept away, and the golden treasure was melted down for shipment back to Spain.

The fall of the mighty Inca Empire before this laughably tiny band of adventurers seems incredible, and in some ways it was. But if we examine it more closely, we can find some reasons for it. The Spanish soldiers were fearless, indeed downright fanatical in their quest. Their desire to spread the Christian religion to the heathen and find gold had somehow merged and the quest for golden riches had become a religious act. The Spainards didn't have many guns, but on the other hand, the Indians didn't have any. More important than the guns were the horses. The Indians had never seen horses before, and were genuinely terrified of them.

The real key to Pizarro's success, however, lay in the structure of the Inca Empire. All the power of the empire was in the hands of a single man, the Lord Inca himself. He exercised this power through a small body of officials and priests, generally members of his own family. Such an empire is top-heavy and bound to be unstable. The structure of the Inca Empire was typical of the empires of pre-Conquest South America, and in reconstructing the history of these empires, historians have discovered that they rose and fell with astonishing speed, even before the Spanish arrived. A small tribe or clan could often topple an enormous empire, by simply replacing the group at the top. That is how the Incas themselves had risen to power. For the ordinary people, a change at the top merely meant a change of masters. This time, however, the new masters came from across the sea and they permanently altered an entire way of life for the worse.

In an absolute monarchy one need only depose the monarch, and the system is in great danger. Here Pizarro was supremely lucky, for when he entered the land of Inca, it had just emerged from a civil war in which two rival Lord Incas were contending for power.

The victor in this war, Atahualpa, had not even entered his capital of Cuzco when Pizarro and his little band appeared. Atahualpa had heard rumors of these interesting strangers. The Spanish had been ranging up and down the coast of Peru for years. But the Lord Inca certainly didn't believe he had anything to fear from them. In fact, he thought that they were coming to offer him tribute like other tribes.

Pizarro invited Atahualpa to his camp for dinner. So, on November 15, the Lord Inca, accompanied by six thousand unarmed warriors, entered the Spanish camp at Cajamarca. One of the Spaniards recalled later that the Lord Inca, atop a palanquin borne on the shoulders of his nobles, "gleamed like a castle of gold."

The Spaniards had prepared a surprise attack for their all-too-trusting guest. At the cry, "Santiago and at them," Spaniards rushed from their hiding places, their guns and horses spreading confusion and panic among the soldiers and servants of the Lord Inca. Within half an hour two thousand Inca warriors had been killed and Atahualpa himself captured, though his unarmed men fought desperately to save him. The Spaniards' losses were negligible. The major battle of the conquest had been won.

Ultimately the Indians recovered from their initial shock. They learned how to cope with the muskets and the horses, and even to ride horses when they could capture some from the Spanish. They fought fiercely for years. But it was too late, for the Spanish had secured their power. Though the Spanish suffered many heavy losses in the battles that followed, they could never be dislodged.

The fate of the captured Atahualpa brings us back to gold. The Lord Inca knew that the Spaniards wanted gold, and so in return for his life he offered them a treasure of almost unimaginable worth. He stretched his arm above his head and asked his captors to draw a line on the wall where his fingers touched. He then offered to fill the room with gold up to the line in return for his release. The room was twenty-five feet long and fifteen feet wide. The line was a bit more than seven feet off the floor.

Pizarro agreed to the proposition, though it is doubtful if he ever had any intention of releasing Atahualpa. Free, the Lord Inca would become a dangerous enemy who could rally his people against the invaders. The Spaniards didn't think the Inca could gather that much gold. But they had not counted on the wealth of the Inca Empire and the efficiency of its communications.

Runners were sent out to the farthest part of the empire, and very soon the roads were filled with men carrying *cargas* litters slung on long poles. The *cargas* were filled with gold, and some were so heavy that it took four men to lift them.

There were sheets of gold ripped from temples, golden vessels of every size and shape, ornaments and utensils from the temples and royal palaces, golden statues of people and animals. The skill of the Inca craftsmen could be seen in golden imitations of Indian corn, in which the golden ear was sheathed in broad leaves of silver from which hung a rich tassel of threads of the same precious metal. According to a contemporary report, there was also a fountain "which sent up a sparkle jet of gold, while birds and animals of the same material played in the waters at its base."

Contrary to a widely repeated version of this event, the golden treasure never did quite fill the room to a height of seven feet. Atahualpa had promised the room would be filled in two months. Five months later the room had still not been filled. Some of Atahualpa's enemies in the recent civil war may have been holding back. Still, the amount of gold gathered was enormous, a total of 1,326,539 gold pesos, according to Spanish accounts. It's hard to give a modern equivalent of this, but it was somewhere around 200 million dollars, perhaps more. And, if the Spanish had not melted down most of the golden objects, the treasure of the Inca would have been beyond human reckoning.

Pizarro had the Lord Inca brought to trial and condemned to death. Among the charges brought against him was one stating that he was a worshipper of idols, and his sentence was death by burning, the usual fate of heretics. When Atahualpa learned that his body was to be consumed by fire, which in his religion would have damned him utterly in his life after death, he agreed to become a Christian. For this he was granted the kindness of being garroted like a common criminal.

Some Spaniards today object to the revulsion with which history has viewed the acts of Pizarro and the other conquistadors. They call it "the Black Legend" and say that all the stories of greed and cruelty are exaggerated, and that other peoples would have acted the same way given similar opportunities. That may be a defense of sorts, but there can be no denying the essential facts of greed and cruelty. The conquistadors kept voluminous records of their activities, and their own words are testimony against them.

The enormous amount of gold collected by Pizarro presents a somewhat deceptive picture. It sounds as though South America was bursting with gold. But, in fact, South America didn't possess a great deal of gold, and never had. What Pizarro, and to a lesser extent Cortes, were able to do was grab, in one swoop, the gold that had been collected by a succession of Indian empires for centuries.

For the moment, though, the gold of the Incas made Pizarro's soldiers rich beyond the dreams of avarice. But prices went up accordingly. Horses in the New World cost from 2,500 to 3,300 gold pesos, a jar of wine cost 60 pesos, and even a string of garlic fetched half a peso. One chronicler of the expedition wrote, "If one man owed anything to another, he paid it in a lump of gold without weighing the gold, and being quite indifferent whether it was worth double the amount of the debt or not."

One of Pizarro's officers, Hernando de Soto was so awed by what he had seen that he set off following rumors of another gold-rich Indian civilization, a place called the Seven Cities of Cibola.

This legend, for that's what it turned out to be, has an interesting origin. It gives us some idea of how men's eyes can be blinded, and their reason befuddled by the glare of gold. The legend of the Seven Cities had not begun in the New World at all. It was around long before Columbus sailed. In its original form, the legend was set, during the Muslim conquest of the Iberian peninsula (Spain and Portugal) in the eighth century. It told of how seven Christian bishops had gathered their flocks and fled by boat to an island in the Atlantic. There they founded seven cities, one for each bishop. For hundreds of years the Island of the Seven Cities appeared on maps made in Europe, though none of the map-makers seemed quite sure where the island was supposed to be or exactly what shape it was.

In 1447 a Portuguese ship reported landing on an island "where the people spoke the Portuguese tongue and asked if the Moors did yet trouble Spain." Most intriguingly, this report said that the people of the Island of the Seven Cities used large gold crucifixes and candlesticks and had altar clothes embroidered with gold thread. When the Portuguese sailors prepared to depart, they noticed that the sand on the beach contained gold dust. Naturally, a lot of mariners set out to find this gold-rich island. None of them ever did, though there were plenty of rumors that someone had, but was keeping it a secret.

Columbus believed firmly in the story of the Island of the Seven Cities. He had hoped to use the island for a staging point for his voyage to the Orient. The island wasn't where he had expected it to be, or anywhere else.

When the conquistadors heard rumors of a cluster of gold-rich cities in what is now the southwestern United States they immediately dubbed them the Seven Cities of Cibola. This was not the only case in which an Old World legend was transported to the New World. Tales of the Amazons, fierce warrior women, were originally placed in Africa. The Spanish reset the legend in South America and from it the Amazon River got its name. The Virgin Islands got their name, not from the Virgin Mary, or the

Virgin Queen (Elizabeth I) as is commonly supposed, but from an old Spanish tale about an armada of ships carrying a thousand virgins who were supposed to be sailing around the Mediterranean looking for husbands. The Spaniards, it appears, hated to give up a good story.

In his search for the Seven Cities of Cibola, de Soto and his men wandered over half the North American continent. They made many important discoveries and were probably the first Europeans to see the Mississippi River. De Soto himself died during their wanderings, and was buried in the Mississippi. But the expedition never found the Seven Cities or any other golden cities. The Indians of North America were gold poor in comparison with the Indians of South America.

Francisco Pizarro's younger brother Gonzago became involved in the search for one of the most haunting and enduring of golden legends, that of El Dorado, the golden man.

The story that reached the ears of Spanish in Mexico and Peru was that there was a land high in the mountains where once a year, at sunrise, the people performed the ceremony, *el hombre dorado.* During the ceremony, the king would cover his body with a sticky substance, and then have gold dust sprinkled upon him. Before dawn the golden king would be rowed out to the center of the sacred lake. As the first rays of the sun struck his golden body, the king would dive into the water, and swim to shore, now washed clean of the gold. The people on the shore would cheer and toss their own golden ornaments into the lake as a sacrifice.

As a matter of fact, this particular story happened to

be true. The sacred lake was Lake Guatavita, high on the plateau of Cundinamarca, north of modern Bogata, Colombia. The people who held the ceremony were the Chibchas, a fairly advanced tribe, but in no way comparable to the highly developed societies of the Incas and Aztecs.

The Spanish had assumed that any people that could afford such a prodigal waste of gold must be incomparably rich in the metal. What they had failed to consider was the fact that it doesn't really take a great deal of gold dust to cover a man's body. Besides, the Chibchas had abandoned the ceremony years before the Spanish had ever heard of it.

In 1529, even before Pizarro's conquest of Peru, men had begun searching for the land of El Dorado. Over the years dozens of expeditions struck out in all directions, into the mountains, into the jungles, and into the swamps. Some were never heard from again. As an almost accidental byproduct of the El Dorado search, the entire length of the Amazon River was explored by men from Gonzago Pizarro's expedition. The searchers subjected themselves to hideous, almost unbelievable hardships; and inflicted hideous and almost unbelievable cruelties on the Indians through whose lands they passed.

Actually the land of El Dorado, that is, the plateau of Cundinamarca, was discovered in 1537, quite early in the El Dorado story. It was reached almost simultaneously by three separate expeditions that had started out from different places and were unknown to one another. The first of the expeditions to reach the land was led by Gonzalo Jiménez de Quesada. There remained less than two hundred ragged, half-starved survivors of an expedition that started with over seven hundred men and very high hopes.

The plateau of Cundinamarca had no gold of its own. The Chibchas obtained what little gold they did possess by trading salt, their chief export, for gold from the neighboring tribes. They had given up the El Dorado ceremony because it was a waste of scarce gold.

De Quesada was able to collect only about two hundred pounds of golden ornaments and decorations in the land of El Dorado. Because there was so little gold he refused, in the face of all evidence, to believe that he had found El Dorado, and he went on looking. Thirty years later, when de Quesada was nearly eighty, he was still looking. When de Quesada died, his closest living relative was a niece in Spain. All he had to leave her was his royal grant to look for the land of El Dorado. The niece's husband, Antonio de Berrio, inherited not only de Quesada's grant, but his obsession as well. Berrio searched for another twenty years. It wasn't until the nineteenth century that the dream of El Dorado finally died entirely.

Or, has it really died? Not only did the gold-covered king dive into Lake Guatavita, the people on the shore also threw in some of their golden ornaments. So, the thinking ran, even though the people were not as wealthy as the Incas, there still must be plenty of gold at the bottom of that lake. A small amount of gold was recovered from the lake, and this has stimulated attempts to dredge, and even drain the entire lake. These efforts have not met with much success, because they are extremely expensive. But every once in a while someone comes up with a new idea about how to get the gold out of El Dorado's lake.

Much of the gold of the New World was loaded onto ships for transport back to Spain. Waiting to seize the treasure ships before they reached Spain were pirates from other nations. This conflict between the pirates, many of whom operated under grants from such countries as England, became sort of an undeclared war that went on for a century.

Besides pirates there was the risk of storms and other hazards of the sea. As a result many of the treasure ships failed to reach their destination. But even with these dangers a seemingly endless stream of gold from the New World flowed into the coffers of the king of Spain, and Spain, temporarily, became the most powerful nation in Europe. For a long time, it was assumed that the prosperity of Spain and Portugal depended primarily on the gold. Modern economic historians no longer accept this thesis. They point out that other commodities brought from the New World and the market for Spanish goods in her overseas colonies made a more substantial basis for prosperity in the Iberian peninsula.

Certainly there were more important products than gold to be found in the New World. Better than half of the vegetables that we commonly eat, including such mainstays as the potato and tomato, were originally imported from South America. The introduction of the potato changed the eating habits of Europe's poor. Chocolate comes from the New World, and so does tobacco.

Yet, today, who thrills to the thought of a potato? It is the "gold of the Indies" that stirs our blood, just as it stirred the blood of the conquistadors four centuries ago.

6

LOST TREASURES

Today treasure hunting is a small but vigorous industry. There are several magazines devoted exclusively to treasure hunting, and each year a number of books on the subject appear. A variety of devices, from simple metal detectors to highly sophisticated instruments for underwater exploration, are offered for sale. There are more than a dozen U.S. companies exclusively devoted to treasure hunting, as well as an unknown number of full-time free-lance treasure hunters. Each year people sink untold hundreds of thousands of dollars into schemes that are supposed to recover this or that sunken galleon, or find a buried treasure.

OSITE: *Diver inspects cannon brought up from the Gulf of Mexico, eved to be from the treasure ship Atocha, sunk in 1607.* (UPI)

Treasure hunting is, at its very best, a financially risky business, and there is a high percentage of just plain fraud in the field. There is almost certainly more spent each year on trying to find treasure, than there is treasure recovered. A lot of treasure hunting is illegal, and most of it is immoral, for it usually involves violating a site of potential historical and archaeological importance for the gold that it contains.

None of this is likely to deter the dedicated treasure hunter. Like other seekers after gold, the quest can become an obsession bordering on madness.

The obsession is hardly a new one, and tales of lost and hidden gold have come down to us from ancient times. The stories of treasure are so encrusted in colorful legend that it is no longer possible to distinguish myth from fact. Indeed, even in more recent ones, the distinction is often difficult to make.

One of the more intriguing tales concerns lost Incan gold. In one form or another this story has been around for several hundred years. It allegedly dates back to the time of Pizarro's capture of Atahualpa. When the word went out that the Lord Inca's subjects were to collect all the gold they could for their lord's ransom, his subjects in what is now Ecuador were slow in gathering their portion. Eventually, though, they did gather a substantial golden treasure. But, as the treasure caravan was on the road to the Spanish, news came that Atahualpa had already been killed.

The Inca nobles of Quinto then diverted their treasure shipment into the eastern Andes. At the headwaters of the Rio Verde in the Llanganati Mountains the Indians dammed a small tributary, thus creating a deep artificial lake. Into this lake they poured the millions of dollars worth of gold that had once been destined to save the life of their murdered king.

The location of this artificial lake was known to very few, among them an Indian princess who later married a Spaniard named Valverde and revealed the secret to him. Upon his death Valverde bequeathed the secret of this lost treasure to the king of Spain. The king sent his agents to Ecuador to try to locate the treasure, but Valverde's instructions had been very inexact and they could find nothing.

Others have searched for the spot known as the Dorrotero of Valverde, with an equal lack of success. Was Valverde's information too vague, or is it possible that he was given false information entirely? Is it possible that there never was any lost treasure of the Incas in the first place? Nobody really knows.

Over the centuries many treasure-bearing ships have gone to the bottom, taking their treasure with them. The *Atocha* was only one of them, but one that has recently been in the news. The ship was part of a Spanish convoy that went down in a hurricane off the Florida Keys in 1622. The total loss was 550 Spaniards, an uncounted number of Indian and black slaves, and an enormous amount of gold and silver. According to documents in the Spanish archives in Seville, the *Atocha* had carried 901 silver ingots, 250,000,000 freshly minted silver coins, and 161 pieces of gold bullion. There were also the personal belongings of the rich merchants aboard, and an unknown but very probably large quantity of gold and silver contraband being smuggled out of the New World.

Attempts to salvage the *Atocha's* treasure began almost immediately after the sinking. The ship had gone down in fifty feet of water, and at first the stump of a mast still broke the waves. But a second hurricane wiped out that marker.

The early Spanish salvage attempts used grappling hooks, a primitive diving bell, and a large number of professional pearl divers. The attempts went on for decades and cost the lives of many divers, but they were completely unsuccessful. Finally the wreck of the *Atocha* was forgotten. Written records of its cargo, sinking, and the attempts to salvage it gathered dust in the archives in Seville, Spain. Then in the mid-1960s a researcher for the Smithsonian Institution found a reference to the ship. A list of lost treasure ships compiled by the Spanish put the *Atocha* right at the top.

That led searchers to Seville to look at the original records. These, however, were difficult to decipher, for they had been handwritten in an ink that had faded over the centuries. Worse still, the names of some of the places in the Florida Keys had changed. No one really knew where to look. A dozen treasure-hunting groups, each working with copies of the original report, were unable to locate the *Atocha* though they searched for five years. A reexamination of the original records by an associate of treasure hunter Mel Fisher indicated that everyone had been looking one hundred miles to the west of the actual wreck site. Fisher moved his team to the new location and quickly found what appeared to be the remains of a Spanish ship. But was it the treasure ship?

The first major find, an eight-foot-gold chain, was

made by a diver named Don Kincaid, who said, "I thought it was brass, or that somebody had tossed it in to fool me, the new guy. But it was pretty heavy for brass." Then he showed it to his companions on the surface, and, he reported, "It was pandemonium . . . Gold fever swept the whole boat."

The chain had links measuring about three eighths of an inch each, each link corresponding in weight to a specific unit of the 1622 currency. Some Spanish merchant had apparently been carrying his money home to Spain around his neck when the ship was sunk. Fisher appraised the chain at $120,000.

But a single find, however valuable, did not mean that they had found the *Atocha* or the treasure. The remains of the wreck were scattered over approximately a square mile of sea bottom. The timbers had long since disappeared; only metal, porcelain, and the stones used for ballast would remain. (Since the ship had been at the bottom only 350 years, most of the other metals, including gold, would have survived.)

The chain was found in 1971. It was two more years before another significant find was made. This was a silver bar that definitely could be traced to the cargo of the *Atocha*. It wasn't until 1975 that anything else of interest was found. Then the ship's nine cannons were located.

On July 19, 1975, shortly after the discovery of the cannons, tragedy struck the treasure hunters. Since treasure hunters are chronically short of money, they can rarely maintain their boats in top condition. One of Fisher's boats capsized, drowning three of those on board. Two of the dead were Fisher's own children. A fourth diver had been killed earlier when sucked into the propeller of a boat.

Financial troubles were also mounting. Despite the finds and the prospects of greater finds to come, Fisher and his crew were having troubles making ends meet. In his treasure-hunting career, Mel Fisher claimed he had found millions, but between expenses and taxes he lived like a poor man. A government agency was still looking into his financial dealings.

When writer Robert Daly visited Fisher in late summer, 1975, he found ". . . Fisher's wife Deloris, who had once set the woman's underwater endurance record—more than 55 hours without coming up—but who now, mourning over her first-born son, was on the edge of hysteria all the time. He was forever having to take her aside and put his arms around her."

Yet, he was going on with the project. And he assured Daly with the optimism that is so essential to all treasure hunters, that within a week or two he was sure to locate the *Atocha's* main treasure hold, and then everything was going to work out. By early 1976 the main body of the treasure still had not been located, and the search goes on.

Advances in technology, particularly in underwater diving equipment and metal detectors have made possible, though not necessarily profitable, what was impossible just a few decades ago. The scent of sunken treasure may bring a dozen or so different treasure-hunting parties to a region within a matter of days. It will also attract a number of government inspectors, eager to claim their share of whatever is found.

The legal status of sunken treasure is often unclear. Some nations claim all of a treasure if the vessel is found off their coast. In the United States the legal status of treasure brought up off the coast varies greatly from state to state, and sometimes from case to case. Florida, off whose coast many treasure-bearing wrecks like the *Atocha* are presumed to lie, strictly regulates treasure hunting. Licenses cost six hundred dollars each and cover a specific area of eighteen square miles for a year. The treasure hunters are also required to put up a five-thousand-dollar bond to assure the state that it will get a share of anything they find. The state usually claims 25 percent of everything of value brought to the surface.

The absolute value of a piece of treasure is impossible to determine. One can easily find the value of the gold itself by checking the price for the day on the London gold market. But the value of a golden object may far outweigh the value of the gold itself. The contents of many treasure ships have been sold on the black market, for treasure hunters often do not wish to reveal the source of their find since that would stimulate competition and attract the attention of government authorities. But they also frequently circulate stories that exaggerate the amount they have received for their treasure. This might seem unwise for people who don't want to attract attention. But treasure hunters, who always need cash, must also attract investors with visions of the riches to be reaped if only they back this latest venture.

In November of 1975 a Golden Galleon Treasure Sale was held at the Waldorf-Astoria Hotel in New York. A single coin, a gold doubloon struck at Mexico City in 1702, went for $21,500. Mel Fisher once said, "If I say a piece of treasure is worth something, then that's what it's worth. You can't get it anywhere else for less."

Archaeologists and historians deplore the whole treasure-hunting business. They contend that treasure hunters destroy much of the historical value of any find in their grab for the gold. Some of the larger treasure-hunting companies have tried to make their peace with the archaeologists, and combine treasure hunting with science. This venture has not been entirely successful. Most marine archaeologists and historians are still calling for a complete ban on treasure-hunting activities off the U.S. coast. Such a ban would doubtless be a boon to archaeology and history, but a loss to romance and adventure.

In recent years much of the popular attention has been focused on sunken treasures. But, to my mind at least, there is nothing that quite matches the allure of buried treasure. Perhaps that is a notion that grew out of reading Robert Louis Stevenson's classic, *Treasure Island.* Buried treasures are not nearly as common in fact as they have been in fiction. But there have been some real buried treasures, and hints and rumors of many, many more.

The notorious Blackbeard the pirate is said to have stashed much of his ill-gotten gains on Amelia Island, some thirty miles north of Jacksonville, Florida. You can still buy "treasure maps" showing where Blackbeard was supposed to have buried the treasure. Why don't the people selling the maps go dig up the treasure themselves? Simple, the maps are fake. No one has yet found Blackbeard's treasure.

Cocos Island, off the Pacific coast of Costa Rica, is reputed to contain no less than three separate treasure hordes. According to tradition, two pirates, Captain Edward Davis and Benito Bonito, buried treasure on Cocos during the eighteenth century. Davis's treasure is said to have consisted of seven hundred bars of gold, twenty water kegs filled with gold doubloons, and more than one hundred tons of Spanish silver reals. Bonito's horde was a hundred and fifty tons of gold taken from a Spanish ship he captured off the coast of Acapulco, Mexico. He is also said to have buried several members of his mutinous crew with the treasure.

Most attention, however, has focused on the "Treasure of Lima," for which the evidence is somewhat more substantial. In 1821 Spanish colonial rule in Peru was being threatened by the revolutionary forces of Simon Bolivar. The church and municipal authorities of Lima decided to get all the city's portable wealth out of the way of the rebels. Most of the wealth was gold taken from Lima's churches. They hired an English brig called the *Mary Dier*, captained by one Charles Thompson, to take the treasure to Panama for safekeeping with the Spanish officials there.

Captain Thompson, however, was unable to resist the lure of the gold, so instead of sailing to Panama, he made for Cocos Island where he hid the treasure, and drew a map showing the hiding place.

What happened after that is not really clear. The *Mary Dier* seems to have been sunk, but Thompson survived. He turned up in Newfoundland, still clutching his map. He didn't survive in Newfoundland for long, though, and died under conveniently mysterious circumstances.

The map then passed into the hands of a couple of Newfoundlanders called Boag and Keating. They set out for Cocos, but once again the curtain drops. A few months later a Newfoundland whaler stopped at Cocos, and found that it contained only one living resident, Keating. Keating said the crew of his ship had mutinied and stranded both him and Boag, and that Boag had later died of a "fever." Keating returned to Newfoundland, with the map, but without the treasure.

When he died in 1873 he left the map to a man named Fitzgerald, who didn't go treasure hunting himself but was happy to sell copies of his map to those who wanted to.

After that, dozens of treasure hunts were staged but they were not easy. Cocos has a horrible climate, and is infested with noxious insects. One treasure hunter said the island reminded him of a grave. Most expeditions were driven off within a few days or weeks.

Why, with the aid of a map, are people still unable to locate the treasure on a small island? One possible reason is that the map is a fake, that the story of the Treasure of Lima is a fake, and that there is no gold at all on Cocos Island. Treasure hunters don't like to think about that possibility. Another possibility is that the violent tropical storms and earthquakes that frequently strike Cocos obliterated the landmarks shown on the original map. And at least one gold horde, and quite possibly all three, still await the lucky finder. Many still try and Costa Rica makes a tidy sum by selling licenses to hunt treasure on Cocos Island.

So far we have been talking about treasures that can't be found. But what is unquestionably the strangest and most intriguing treasure story of modern times concerns a treasure whose location has been known for nearly two centuries but which cannot be recovered.

That story begins on a morning in October, 1795. Three boys were paddling their canoe across Mahone Bay, on the southern shore of Nova Scotia. They put in at Oak Island, one of the 350 small islands in the bay. It is about three quarters of a mile long and a mile wide, and even then was often used as a picnic spot. In a clearing on the island the boys found a large oak tree that bore the unmistakable signs of having been used to anchor a rope and tackle. Beneath the tree was a circular depression that looked as though something had been buried there.

The boys had heard all about pirates and buried treasure. Captain Kidd had once sailed the waters around Nova Scotia. Naturally they began digging in the hard clay. Ten feet down they struck a platform made of solid oak logs. Convinced that a treasure lay just beneath this barrier, they broke through the logs, only to find that there was more hard clay underneath. A few feet farther down the boys unearthed a rusty boatswain's whistle, and a copper coin dated 1713.

Ten feet under the first wooden platform, they struck a second, and ten feet farther down, a third. That was about all they could accomplish with the tools they had, but they didn't give up and two of them actually moved to Oak Island. It was years before they were able to attract enough interest in the Oak Island treasure to purchase excavating equipment to do a proper job.

As the diggers went down they hit identical wooden platforms every ten feet.

At ninety-three feet they came upon a layer of charcoal, ship's putty, and mats of coconut fiber, a material not native to Oak Island. Under that was a large flat stone that contained odd markings. It has often been said that the markings read, "Two Million Pounds Lie Buried Ten Feet Below." But that translation is certainly false, if for no other reason than the fact that in those days any amount of money would have been stated in guineas rather than in pounds. The stone slab was removed and no one paid much attention to it. It disappeared during the 1920s and the story of the inscription has grown since.

After the diggers had reached a depth of ninety-five feet and removed the stone slab, they took a day off. When they returned they found that the hole they dug was filled with sixty feet of water, and no matter how hard they bailed, they couldn't empty it.

This first major attempt to locate the Oak Island treasure went down defeated. In 1849 a group of Nova Scotia businessmen formed a well-financed syndicate. They sunk a drill into the hole. At ninety-eight feet, three feet deeper than the original excavation, the drill passed through another layer of oak and then penetrated what appeared to be loose metal. Brought to the surface, the drill bit was found to contain two tiny links of a golden chain. There seemed to be a wooden chest containing gold down in the hole. Further drilling located evidence of another wooden chest, just beneath the first.

Now, it might seem that all one had to do was go

down and pull out the treasure. But there was the water to contend with, and no one knew where it was coming from. Close inspection of the area revealed that whoever had dug the pit in the first place had also dug an underwater channel to the beach. It was so arranged that if anyone tried to dig down into the treasure pit it would automatically fill with water, which was exactly what had happened. There must have been some means of shutting the water off so that those who had hidden the treasure in the first place could get it out. But no one has ever been able to discover by what method this could be done.

The Nova Scotia syndicate ran out of money. Others took up the search with no more success. In 1893 another major and well-financed attempt was made. This group drilled even deeper. At 151 feet the drill hit a layer of concrete, and under it evidence of another metal-filled chest. At 170 feet the drill hit an obstruction it could not penetrate, a metal plate. The plate may have formed the floor of the pit, or may have been the cover for still more treasure below. No one has ever gone deeper. Many have speculated that the two chests buried at 100 feet are merely decoys, and that the real treasure lies beneath the concrete and the metal.

The diggers managed to block off the channel that brought in sea water, only to discover that there was a second one, and the hole again filled up with water. All the digging, drilling, and water had turned the whole area into a quagmire, and this expedition, too, went broke, defeated by the mud and water.

Expedition followed expedition. Perhaps the most

expensive to date was launched in 1935. This group managed to get the hole pumped out all right, but could do nothing about the mud. Much worse was the discovery that the mud in the hole had shifted so much that the chests could no longer be located with a drill. The diggers were playing a game of blind man's bluff in the mud. Another failure. Yet another group took up the challenge in 1970. At this writing they are still at it.

The treasure, whatever it is, is still there today. If you want to go look at the site it's easy enough, for thousands of tourists visit Oak Island each year to stare down what has come to be called the Money Pit. Whether this name is for the money that is supposed to be in the hole, or for the money that has been poured into the attempt to get the treasure out, is unclear. The area now looks as though it has been bombed. It is strewn with abandoned mining equipment, and, one may assume, abandoned dreams.

To this day no one knows who built the Money Pit or what it is protecting. The whole conception seems too sophisticated for pirates. One theory is that the pit was built by the French who had hidden a treasure there when they feared attack by the British. The French military engineers were the best in the world and would have possessed the skill to design such a hiding place. But there isn't a hint of this in any of the French records, and that is rather strange.

The treasure could almost certainly be gotten out of the hole with an unlimited expenditure of time and money, and perhaps a little luck. But such ventures must be undertaken by large financial syndicates, and they don't have the romantic spirit of the lone treasure hunter. There are profit and loss sheets to be figured out, and stockholders to be considered. There are easier ways for people with money to make more money from gold.

7

GOLD RUSHES

There is nothing quite like the cry of "Gold!" to drive men half-mad and send them rushing across a continent, or round the world. They will leave behind home and family, abandon all ordinary or even minimal comforts, endure incredible hardships, face death dozens of times each day, and still continue to hope for success in the face of all evidence to the contrary. It has also, not infrequently, turned normally decent folk into cheats, thieves, and murderers.

The event that led to the popularity of the term, gold rush, was the discovery of gold in California in 1849. But that was certainly not the first gold rush in history

OSITE: *Sutter's Mill, site of the first major gold find in California.*
w York Public Library Picture Collection)

nor, in fact, the first in North America. The first major gold find in North America was made by a twelve-year-old boy named Conrad Reed who lived in North Carolina in 1799. The boy found a pretty yellow rock in a stream near his home, but he had no idea what it was. His family kept the rock around for a few years, and finally sold it to a jeweler for $3.50. The rock turned out to be a gold nugget weighing seventeen pounds and was eventually resold for 4,000 dollars, an enormous sum of money in the early 1800s.

When word of this discovery got around, gold hunters flocked to the area, and they did find plenty of gold. So much in fact, that the U.S. mint built a branch in nearby Charlotte, North Carolina, and turned out 55 million dollars worth of gold coins.

But the California discovery is much more famous, and justifiably so. It produced more gold, generated more misery and hardship, and quite literally changed the face of America.

The story began on a rainy day in January, 1848, at the office of John Augustus Sutter, a wealthy Swiss farmer who had migrated to California and obtained a huge land grant from the Mexican government, which at that time controlled California. Standing in the rain outside Sutter's door was his foreman, James W. Marshall. Sutter was not expecting to see Marshall, and motioned him inside.

The foreman was acting very strangely. He indicated that he had something to tell Sutter in private. When the two men were alone Marshall pulled a pea-sized yellow nugget out of his pocket, and announced that he had found gold in a stream where a sawmill for Sutter's timber was being constructed.

Sutter had failed to lock the door, and during the conversation one of the clerks popped his head in and mumbled something about having been away from his desk. Perhaps the clerk had heard the magic word, gold, through the door, and decided to look in to see what was going on.

Oddly, neither Sutter nor Marshall was particularly elated by the discovery. Sutter was already an extremely wealthy man, and Marshall had been promised a share of the profits from the sawmill, which could be considerable. Both men knew that a horde of gold hunters descending upon the land would completely alter whatever plans they had for the future. Then, there was a certain amount of anxiety over the property itself. In less than two weeks the territory of California was due to be turned over to the United States. What would be the fate of Sutter's grant then, particularly if gold were found?

The two men determined to keep the news secret, at least for a couple of weeks until the mill was finished, and the new authority of the United State government firmly established. But the secret was already out. The nosy clerk had overheard the conversation. Would history have been any different if Sutter had remembered to lock the door, and he and Marshall had talked more quietly? Probably not. The workmen on the mill had also seen the gold, and though Sutter begged them to keep quiet, they didn't.

Sutter's own agent went to San Francisco to confirm

land claims with the new government, carrying some gold dust with him. Within a few weeks, San Francisco, a sleepy little port town in 1848, had practically emptied out. A man named Thomas O. Larkin wrote to the secretary of state in Washington of the fever that gripped California over the next few months. "This town of San Francisco has one half of its tenements empty, locked up with the furniture; the owners, storekeepers, lawyers, mechanics, and laborers are all gone to the Sacramento [the town nearest Sutter's find] with their families."

One of San Francisco's two newspapers had to suspend publication entirely after its whole staff decamped to the gold fields. The other limped along in irregular fashion with a staff of one holdout.

News, even news of a gold strike, didn't travel quite as quickly in 1848 as it does today. But it did travel, first throughout California, then all the way across the North American continent. As far east as Nantucket Island, thirty miles off the coast of Massachusetts, where a large percentage of the men were engaged in the dirty and hazardous business of whaling, the news inspired men to try their luck in the California gold fields. They promptly set sail, leaving Nantucket in almost total possession of women and children. The men of Nantucket were actually in better shape to make the trip than many others. They had the ships.

There were no jets, automobiles, railroads, and no Panama Canal in 1848. The easiest, safest, and fastest way to get from the East Coast to the West Coast was to sail all the way around Cape Horn, the tip of South America. At that the trip was no picnic. It covered eighteen thousand miles, and took at least five months, if you were lucky. What with storms, rocks, unseaworthy vessels, and all the other dangers attendant upon long voyages in small ships, there was a chance that you would not arrive at all. Besides, the trip was expensive.

An intermediate and somewhat cheaper journey was to sail to Panama, then travel by canoe, on muleback, or on foot across the Isthmus of Panama to the Pacific side, where you would board another ship. It was a short, danger-filled trip through jungle country containing everything, including cannibals.

Only those who could not afford the price of the voyage, and that was the majority, tried to walk or ride (mostly walk) from one coast to the other over three thousand miles. The ordinary dangers of difficult and unknown country and hostile Indians were amplified by the poverty of most of these forty-niners, as the gold seekers came to be called in honor of the year that they started their trek. They were undersupplied and badly led, if indeed they were led at all. If any extra hardship befell them, they had absolutely no resources to fall back upon.

There was gold in California, of course, lots of it. But not nearly as much as the wild, almost-hysterical accounts that began appearing in newspapers said there was.

The December 6 issue of the Hartfort *Courant* said:

> The California gold fever is approaching its crisis. We are told that the new region that has just become a part of our possessions is El Dorado . . . By a sudden and accidental discovery the ground is

> represented to be one vast gold mine. Gold is picked up in pure lumps, twenty-four carats fine.

The hysteria was fueled by advertisements from shipping companies and others who profited handsomely from this mass movement.

But newspaper accounts, and advertisements, no matter how wild and exaggerated, could not match the visions of infinite riches that the hopeful travelers carried in their heads. Wages in America were about a dollar a day, and the gold hunters had heard of prospectors recovering a thousand dollars in gold a day. The gold fever afflicted not only Americans, it drew Europeans, Chinese, Australians, South Africans, and the natives of a host of other countries to the California gold fields.

In 1850, before the full force of the gold rush had really registered in California, the territory had a population of 92,497. Ten years later the census recorded a population of 379,994; it had more than quadrupled. Not all of the newcomers had been drawn by the lure of gold, but a great number of them had come for just that reason.

Not all those who started for California made it, either. Many died of starvation, thirst, disease or accidents along the way. Others were killed by Indians, by bandits, or their own friends. Still others were drowned in shipwrecks. Some turned back, and many gave up and settled somewhere along the way. It has been said, with considerable justification, that the discovery of gold in California set off one of the great mass movements in human history. It certainly speeded up the development of the American West.

The gold in California was what is called placer gold. It was found mixed with sand or gravel on or near the surface. Thus, it was relatively easy to get at. One very large nugget of almost pure gold weighing 141 pounds 4 ounces was found. Most of the gold, however, was found in the form of dust mixed in with gravel or sand. To extract this gold, most miners used the simple and cheap ancient method of panning. Gold-bearing sand or gravel was placed in a round, high-sided iron pan with a pocket at the bottom. The pan was then rotated under a gentle stream of water. Slowly the lighter gravel or sand was washed away, leaving a small quantity of gold dust in the pocket. The richer the find, the more gold could be extracted with each pan.

Miners who already gained some experience in North Carolina had a better method. They built wooden contraptions called rockers or cradles. These were inclined wooden boxes about three feet long. Strips of wood were fastened across the bottom of the box to catch the gold. Sometimes these gold traps were reinforced with scraps of rough woolen blankets to catch gold particles. Gold-bearing sand and water were poured into the box, which was agitated or rocked gently back and forth. The heavy gold settled on the wooden strips or was trapped in the wool, while the sand and water poured out of the lower end of the box. There were a number of refinements and improvements on the rocker, but the principle remained the same. Indeed, Egyptian miners, thousands of years before, had used very similar methods.

The process was tedious, but if a site was rich in gold dust it could be extremely rewarding. At a place called Tin Cup Diggings, miners could fill a tin cup with gold every day. At Durgan's Flat, one Frank Anderson and three companions took $12,900 in gold dust from a gold pocket in just eleven days.

Most sites weren't nearly that rich, and many miners wandered about for years without finding any appreciable quantity of gold. Besides, what might have looked like a fortune in the East soon melted away in the face of the inflated prices of the gold fields. In San Francisco hotels, bread was selling for a dollar a slice, and potatoes a dollar each. Prospectors weren't teetotalers or cocktail drinkers. They wanted their whisky straight and in great quantity. The prices of even the poorest grades were astronomical. Literally tons of gold dust also passed over the tables in the gambling houses of California. There weren't enough coins or greenbacks to go around and most trading was done in gold dust. A pinch of gold was worth a dollar and men with fat thumbs had an advantage.

The miner who wanted to provision himself for a trip to the gold fields had to put out fifty dollars for a barrel of flour to make his flapjacks, the miner's staple food and usually all he could afford to eat. Salt pork was two hundred dollars a barrel. A candle could run as much as three dollars. Even in today's inflationary times those prices sound high—and in the 1850s flour, under normal conditions, cost under a dollar a barrel.

Very few miners found enough gold dust to keep up with the prices. The ones who really made good were the merchants. The prices of getting products to the mining camps were high, but profits were higher still. Merchants could sell goods for ten times the purchase price. Philip D. Armour used the profits from a small butcher shop at a spot called Placerville to launch a meat-packing empire. John Studebaker started his fortune making wheelbarrows for miners, and wound up owning an industrial empire.

Even those miners who "struck it rich" found the source of their wealth was very perishable. A few years, or even months of intensive exploitation and a gold field was worked out. Mining camps and entire towns that had sprung up overnight were deserted just as quickly, as the prospectors moved on in search of new sources of gold. The landscape of California became dotted with ghost towns.

In ten years it was all over, or very nearly so. Lonely miners still eked out a bare existence, panning tiny quantities of gold from nearly exhausted diggings. Others kept on looking for fresh sources, but no major ones were ever discovered in the state. All in all, the California gold rush produced over 500 million dollars worth of gold. That figure can be misleading. for the gold would be worth many times that today. But there were few millionaire miners.

What of Sutter and Marshall, the two who had really started the whole thing? History proved that their initial fears were justified. The gold hunters wrecked Sutter's mill, cut down his trees, and slaughtered his cattle. His prosperous life as a farmer was a shambles. Sutter did some gold hunting on his own, but was not successful. Finally the state of California granted him a small pension. To the end of his life Sutter wore a ring made from the nugget that Marshall had first presented him.

Marshall came off even more poorly. He didn't find

RESTAURANT
MINERS HOME

any more gold, either. Though today there is a statue in his honor at Coloma, California, during his lifetime he lived in dire poverty on the edge of starvation. When asked to assess the gold rush in which he had played so key a role, he gave the score this way: "Yankeedom, $600,000,000; myself individually, $000,000,000."

Most significantly the California gold rush inspired gold rushes elsewhere.

The first was in Australia. Edward Hammon Hargraves, an Australian, was one of the early forty-niners. He found nothing, and returned to Australia in 1850. There he brashly predicted that he would find gold in a week, and remarkably enough, he did, on a tributary of the Macquaire River not far from Bathurst in New South Wales. Hargraves had observed that the terrain of the area resembled that of the California gold fields.

This discovery didn't start an immediate gold rush because people didn't really believe the story. Besides, the British government wasn't particularly anxious to encourage a gold rush. Australia, you see, was a British penal colony, where prisoners outnumbered nonprisoners by about nine to one. The government was afraid that the lure of gold would sharpen the prisoners' natural desire to escape. But, finally, when a seventy-five pound nugget was discovered, people began to believe and flocked to New South Wales in such numbers that Australia's other provinces were alarmed.

Victoria, a neighboring province, lost nearly half its meager population to the gold rush. The government offered a substantial reward to anyone who could find gold within two hundred miles of its capital city. Almost at once prospectors began picking up nuggets the size

OSITE: *Dawson at the height of the Klondike gold rush.* (Library
Congress)

of hens' eggs to the north and west of the city. Nuggets were the specialty in this region. The most spectacular was the monster nugget called the Welcome Stranger, discovered by John Deason and Richard Oates on the afternoon of February, 15, 1869. The men were trying to dig their cart out of a mudhole when their shovels struck a glittering rock. The rock turned out to be nearly solid gold.

It was a mere twenty-one inches long and ten inches thick, but it weighed 2,280 ounces, or close to 150 pounds, and broke the cart in which Deason and Oates tried to move it.

These discoveries had all taken place in Australia's eastern provinces. The western provinces also longed for a gold rush that would bring them prosperity, and they too began offering rewards for the discovery of gold. And gold was discovered. But there was a problem. In California, and most other places, the gold dust was found in or near a water supply. In western Australia, it was discovered in some of the most barren desert regions in the world. The prospectors had trouble getting water to drink; they certainly didn't have enough to wash the gold-bearing sand by any of the traditional methods. So they improvised. One variation of panning was called dry blowing. The miner would place one pan or dish at his feet, fill another with gold-bearing sand, and lift it over his head. He would then slowly pour the contents from one to the other. The wind—there was plenty of wind in the desert—would blow away the lighter sand, allowing the gold to fall into the bottom pan. The process worked, after its fashion, but it was incredibly slow and tedious.

The shaker was a desert variation of the rocker. Instead of a stream of water flowing through the box, it had a bellows attachment that blew a stream of air that separated sand from gold.

Ingenious as these methods were, and hardy as the prospectors were in enduring desert conditions, the gold finds in Western Australia didn't really set off a gold rush until 1892. Then John Ford and Arthur Bayley discovered both gold and water at Coolgardie. That began yet another Australian gold rush.

Back in America, the gold fever didn't disappear simply because the California finds petered out. Prospectors now began searching for the "mother lode." It was assumed that all the loose gold, the gold dust and nuggets, had been washed down from some rich vein of gold high in the mountains. In fact, in many cases the vein of gold from which the gold dust had come may have eroded away entirely millenia ago. But the hope was always there, and sometimes it was rewarded.

In 1858 Patrick McLaughlin and Peter O'Riley, a couple of hard-luck prospectors, were working in an east spur of the Sierras in what was later to become the state of Nevada. The dirt they passed through their rockers yielded an enormous quantity of the gold and silver alloy that the ancients had called electrum. Tracing the alloy to its source, they found it to be a barren hump called, appropriately enough, Gold Hill.

Astonishingly, the forty-niners who gave the hill its name knew that it contained silver. But they were in such a hurry to reach the fabled riches of California, that they passed it up as unworthy. McLaughlin and O'Riley didn't scorn it. Neither did a man named Henry

"Pancake" Comstock, who made himself a partner of the two discoverers, because he controlled the water supply.

McLaughlin and O'Riley wanted to call their find Ophir, after the fabled source of King Solomon's gold. Comstock wanted to name it after himself, and he prevailed. The Comstock Lode, as the discovery was finally called, turned out to be one of the richest single silver finds in history. In the twenty years that the mines of the Comstock Lode were worked, the value of the gold and silver that they yielded was more than half as much as the value of the gold found in all of California. Those overeager forty-niners who had passed right by Gold Hill had no idea of the riches beneath their feet. There were many major silver discoveries in the western United States, but that metal has never possessed the appeal or romance of gold.

More gold was found in the western mountains, but not in any great quantity. What happened at Pike's Peak was typical. A rumor started that gold had been found there. In fact, it hadn't; a nearby find that was responsible for the rumor was of extremely poor quality, barely worth working. Yet, a regular gold fever developed, as novice miners set off with the words "Pike's Peak Or Bust" pinned to their knapsacks. Many, however, returned within a few months wearing a sign that read "Busted."

The fantasy of gold at Pike's Peak was encouraged by outfitters who had become rich selling overpriced supplies to the forty-niners. The outfitters started a regular stagecoach service from Missouri to Denver, then little more than a cluster of shacks, and a hundred miles from Pike's Peak, to boot. Gold really was discovered at Cripple Creek at the base of Pike's Peak in 1891. That was of little use to those who came looking for it in 1858.

The next really hysterical gold rush came in the 1890s, in the Yukon territory of Western Canada and neighboring Alaska. Some gold had been discovered in the region as early as 1869. But the find that really touched off the rush was not made until 1896, in a stream called the Thron Diuck, which in Indian meant "plenty of fish." The prospectors could never pronounce the name correctly so the place became famous as the Klondike. When the news got around practically all the prospectors in the area moved en masse to the spot, and almost overnight, built a new town, Dawson.

News out of this remote and frozen region traveled slowly. In July, 1897, a year after the find had been made, about one hundred miners, each carrying enough gold dust to excite visions of infinite riches in others, arrived in San Francisco. Soon everyone was talking about the gold strike. There was less talk of those miners who had starved, or gone mad from isolation, or lost fingers and toes to frostbite, or simply frozen to death entirely. The Klondike has a fierce climate, where temperatures of 80° below zero were not uncommon.

The gold rush didn't really get started until the following year, for a trip must be planned long in advance. If the traveler started too late, he risked being quite literally frozen in his tracks.

The easiest way to get to the Klondike gold fields (if any way could be called easy) was to take a ship to the port of St. Michael and then up the Yukon River to

Dawson itself; but that was expensive. A cheaper way to go was to take a ship to Juneau or Skagway, then travel inland to the Klondike over six hundred miles. There were also mountains in the way. There were two ways to get through the mountains. One was through the White Pass, which was steep, treacherous, and long. Only those who could afford dogs or pack animals made that trip. The Chilkoot Pass was the poor man's route. It was shorter, but steeper—much, much steeper. This pass is a rocky canyon, so terrifying in appearance that many of those who started out took one look at it and turned back. But there were plenty of others, brave enough and foolhardy enough to try. At the height of the gold rush, good weather would find a solid line of men crossing the pass. It was said that if a man lost his place in line, it took him hours to get back in. The dangers of the pass were not imaginary, either. In the summer of '98 seventy men were buried in a single avalanche at the Chilkoot Pass.

Once the pass was crossed, there were still hundreds of miles of difficult and dangerous terrain to traverse. There was not time to look at the scenery either, for the season during which one was reasonably safe from blizzards was short. And once at Dawson, then what? In 1898 thirty thousand gold hunters arrived at Dawson. The town had enough shacks and tents to accommodate four hundred of them. Thousands simply slept in the streets, or—to be more accurate—in the mud.

Getting supplies to Dawson, or any of the other mining towns that sprang up in or near the gold fields was expensive, and the prices for goods were astronomical, even by gold rush standards.

Each new gold field presented its own set of problems. In the Yukon it was the cold. The gold was embedded in the permafrost, that portion of the ground that remains frozen all year round. In order to dig any gold, the miners first had to melt the earth. In the beginning they did this simply by building fires. Later, steam was used to melt the earth.

Gold was discovered in other places in Western Canada and Alaska, and in fact both areas still produce a modest amount of gold yearly. But the greatest gold strike in modern times, indeed in any time in history, was made in South Africa. This discovery still dominates the world gold market today.

A MACHINE DR

8

SOUTH AFRICAN GOLD

Gold was first discovered in South Africa in 1886 by two men named George, George Harrison and George Walker. The pair had been prospectors in Australia, without much success. They decided to try their luck in southern Africa, but until 1886 they found nothing and had to turn back to their old trade of house building.

That's what they were doing when they discovered gold. The two Georges were building a house for the widow Gert Oosthuizen, whose farm was on the high upland veld, or grasslands. It is an area that the Boers, descendants of Dutch settlers in South Africa called the Witwatersrand, or "the ridge of the white waters."

POSITE: *Gold mining in South Africa during the 1920's.* (New
k Public Library Picture Collection.)

The region was studded with rocks called *banket.* That is a Boer word meaning "almond cake," for that is what the rock, made of many fused pebbles, faintly resembles.

The rock found on the surface at the widow Oosthuizen's farm was too crumbly to make good building stone, so the two Georges dug for firmer rock below. The slate-gray rock they found was tinged with particles that gleamed tantalizingly. They crushed the rock and panned it and found the gold that they had sought so long, and until that moment so unsuccessfully. They had discovered the tip of the golden iceberg of the richest source of the precious metal that the world has ever known.

An affidavit from Harrison addressed to Stephanus Johannes Paul Kruger, then president of the Boer republic, is still preserved in the City Museum of Johannesburg, a mining town that sprang up near the find, and has since grown into a major city.

The document reads:

> My name is George Harrison and I come from the newly discovered gold fields Kliprivier, especially from a farm owned by a certain Gert Oosthuizen. I have a long experience as an Australian gold digger and I think it is a payable gold field.

Harrison had no idea how payable it was. He sold his claim for about fifty dollars, and disappeared. Legend has it that he was later killed and eaten by lions.

Oddly President Kruger was not altogether overjoyed to hear that gold had been discovered. His people were farmers and liked it that way. He knew what had happened in other places, and he feared that the country would soon be overrun by an army of foreign gold seekers. In fact, the gold strike profoundly altered the history of South Africa, though not quite in the way Kruger had imagined.

Plenty of gold hunters rushed in. But this wasn't to be another Sutter's mill, or Klondike strike, where the lone miner with a mule, a pan, and pick and shovel could extract a fortune from the ground. The difference lay in the nature of the gold ore to be found in South Africa. There was little gold to be found on or near the surface. Most of the gold-bearing rock lies as much as two miles beneath the surface of the earth.

Despite the enormous quantity of gold to be found in the Witwatersrand Reef, or the Rand, as it is simply called, the gold is still thinly spread. It is found in *banket* a layer of conglomerate rock that looks like grayish asphalt. Only rarely can one see any trace of gold at all in the rock itself. Experienced miners are able to spot gold-bearing rock at once, even without the glimmer of gold flecks. A ton of good ore may yield a mere third of an ounce of gold or less.

Geologists theorize that millions of years ago, the waters of the ocean reached as far as the Rand. Rivers carried gold down from the mountains and deposited it on this shore. Then, in a series of massive upheavals under the earth's crust, the sand of the shore was heated and fused into conglomerate rock, and the entire Rand area was lifted high out of the water, folded and twisted, so that the gold-bearing rock now runs a deep and irregular course under the veld.

Mining gold in South Africa is an extremely expensive operation, and a highly technical one. The real story of the South African gold discoveries is not to be found in the gold fields themselves, but in the work of technicians, the calculations of mining engineers, and the manipulations of millionaire financers.

Because of the difficulties connected with mining and processing South African gold, production in that country started slowly. Two years after the initial discovery, South African gold production accounted for 4.3 percent of the world's gold. That wasn't bad, but only a hint of what was to come.

Within a few years of the discovery, the technical problems and expense of mining gold in the Rand were so great that some predicted the mining industry there would soon collapse under its own weight. But a solution was already at hand. In 1887, three Scotsmen had patented a process that made it easier for the gold to be extracted from ore. The process proved to be perfectly adapted to South African mining operations, and by 1892 15 percent of the world's gold was coming from South Africa. By 1898, South Africa had become the world's leading producer of gold, and has remained so, with only one interruption, since that time.

The sole interruption of South Africa's leadership came during the Boer War at the turn of the century. That was when Britain, which counted South Africa as part of its own empire, fought the Boers who made up the majority of the white inhabitants of South Africa and wanted nothing to do with the British Empire. One of the compelling reasons for Britain's pursuit of the war was a desire to gain control of the gold wealth of South Africa, While the British won the Boer War, it proved to be both a difficult and unpopular conflict. The political strength of the Dutch, who now called themselves Afrikaners, continued to grow even under British rule. South Africa began to pursue an increasingly independent course, until in 1960 a referendum declared South Africa a republic and no longer a member of the British Commonwealth; the vote merely confirmed a situation that had already existed for many years.

The early gold mines had been financed by millionaires who had made their money in diamonds. South Africa also contains the world's richest diamond mines. The diamond millionaires were often conservative men who failed to adequately appreciate the enormous potential of the gold fields under their control. They were making a lot of money doing things in an old-fashioned way and saw no reason to change.

An American mining engineer, W. L. Honnold, proposed that the entire Witwatersrand Reef was a vast bowl of gold-bearing rock that stretched for miles across the veld. By mapping the outcroppings of the rock, Honnold thought that he could determine the outlines of this golden bowl, and could pick appropriate spots at which to drill for new gold.

It was a bold enterprise, and one that did not appeal to the conservative South African owners. But one man, Ernest Oppenheimer, an Englishman who had gone to South Africa and made a fortune in diamonds, liked the idea. Rich as he was, Oppenheimer would never have been able to finance the sort of operation that he had in mind. In the spring of 1917 Oppenheimer went to London, where Honnold arranged a meeting with another American mining engineer with excellent connections in the U.S. financial community.

The American engineer's name was Herbert C. Hoover, who was later to become president of the United States. Hoover was intrigued by the possibility of a gold-bearing reef stretching for hundreds of miles. He also liked the way Oppenheimer outlined the mining company he envisioned to exploit this vast potential. Hoover agreed to bring Oppenheimer's proposal before the financial interests controlled by J. P. Morgan and his family.

The financing was quickly arranged, and in September of 1917 the Anglo American Corporation was formed to dig for gold in South Africa. Over a million dollars came from J. P. Morgan and Co. Morgan and the other investors were richly repaid, for Honnold had been right: A huge gold-bearing arc stretching some 350 miles across the veld could be traced. Not only are the gold supplies of South Africa enormous, they are, as far as gold-mining operations are concerned, fairly predictable.

The total output of South African gold is now controlled by a handful of mining companies, of which Anglo American is the largest and by the South African government. The gold fields of South Africa produce a regular, prearranged quantity of gold, year in year out. There is no possibility of a sudden gold strike or bonanza resulting in a flood of new gold into the market, for this would lower the international price of the metal. Nor is there any chance that the field will suddenly "dry up," forcing the price of gold to skyrocket. Regularity and stability are the watchwords of gold mining in South Africa.

The fact that South Africa is the site of the world's richest gold field has profoundly and permanently affected its history; and ultimately, the presence of so much gold in South Africa may have important effects on the politics of the African continent, and perhaps the entire world. The Dutch, who began settling the southern tip of Africa some two hundred years ago, were farmers, and content to remain farmers. They carved out huge estates, and were able to lead the sort of individualistic, pecularily isolated lives that they preferred. But diamonds, and then gold, changed all of that. The first unlooked-for result was the Boer War. The enormous wealth generated by the gold finds has thrust South Africa, somewhat unwillingly, into the twentieth century. It has leaped from being a nation of farmers to one in which the major sources of income are mining, trade, and industry. It has made a one-time colony into an immensely wealthy and powerful nation, by far the wealthiest and most powerful nation in southern Africa, perhaps in all Africa.

Much of the economic success of South Africa in mining and other areas is based on the use of cheap black labor. It is impossible to understand South African gold mining or anything else about modern South Africa, without looking at the race question. Blacks, or Bantus, as they are called in South Africa, outnumber whites four to one. Yet, the government is totally controlled by the white minority. This was the way governments were normally run in colonial Africa. But, after the Second World War, when South Africa began behaving more like an independent country than a British colony, the ruling Nationalist party came up with a plan called apartheid. It is a complex and often changing system aimed at the complete separation of the two races, ultimately into different territories. Of course, the real aim of apartheid is to maintain the dominance of the white minority, and all the talk of separate development is simply a polite fiction to cover this goal. The government of South Africa is tough and repressive, even to whites who actively oppose its policies.

Throughout Africa, white-dominated regimes have fallen rapidly in the past decade. But South Africa remains firm in its old ways, and there seems little immediate likelihood of its falling. There are two reasons for this: First, in South Africa the whites are still a small minority, but they comprise a far larger percentage of the population than they did in other colonial countries, and they have been there a long time. They regard themselves as Africans and have no European homeland to which they can return.

Second, South Africa is an enormously wealthy and developed country that can easily afford all the weapons it needs to defend its way of life. Though the South African racial policies have been widely, almost universally condemned throughout the world, many Americans, British, French, and others have large investments in the country. The Anglo American corporation is one example, but only one. South Africa has many friends in the United States and elsewhere, both in and out of government. So wealthy and powerful is South Africa that even some of the neighboring black-ruled countries have had to deal with it, though they usually do so very quietly.

South Africa seems to be resting securely on a golden foundation. Yet, if there is such a thing as a tide of history, it is clearly running against South Africa. White regimes that had endured for centuries and just a few decades ago looked completely secure have been swept off the continent. The survival of South Africa in its present form into the next century appears highly improbable.

While some South Africans may dream of total separation of the races, this is clearly impossible, for black labor is essential. Nowhere is this more obvious than in the South African gold-mining industry, which employs 44,000 whites and 370,000 blacks.

The earliest accounts of gold mining that we have indicate it was a horrible task, one relegated to slaves and prisoners. It is still a horrible task today.

Ray Vicker, the *Wall Street Journal* staff member, described his guided tour of a South African deep gold mine in his book *Realms of Gold:*

> At the 3,000-foot level, the cage stopped at a brightly lit tunnel with a railroad track running along its floor. A water pipe snaked along the ceiling on one side. A mine train rolled down the track toward us, followed a switch, and disappeared somewhere into another crosscut. The air was hot and heavy with moisture, and after only a few yards of walking along the track, perspiration coursed off my body.
>
> The crosscut led to the stope or mine face. Here the work area was just high enough to allow crews to crawl forward with their jackhammers, explosives, and shovels. Standing in the cross-

> cut, I peered down the stope. It was no place for anyone with claustrophobia, and I wasn't sure visitors would be allowed to clamber down that forty inch-high passage.

But their guide led them down.

> Crouching on all fours he led the way to the stope. I followed with a squirming hand-crawl to a point where a white miner was directing a crew of two Bantus. There didn't seem to be room enough for the three of them, let alone for the four more in our party . . .
>
> Helmet lights gleamed, providing the only illumination. Noise of the air drills thundered and roared with a staccato cadence in the low passage. One of the blacks balanced a drill with a booted foot as he lay on his back, the handles in his fists. A crouched assistant helped apply pressure on the tool. Wood-and-rock pillars supported the tremendous weight of the rock overhead.

Any sort of mining is hazardous, but there are some special dangers attached to working in the deep gold mines of South Africa. At a depth of three thousand feet, where Vicker observed the mining operation, there was a pressure of four thousand pounds per square inch on the rock roof. Gold mines have been sunk much deeper, some reaching a depth of nearly twelve thousand feet. As the depth increases so does the pressure. For that reason, extreme care must be taken to brace the tunnels in which the men work. Sometimes the pressure is so great that the rock will explode like a bomb, throwing off deadly fragments of rock in all directions. And the mines are hot. The deeper they are, the hotter they are. Even at three thousand feet the tunnels must be air-conditioned, and while still hot, they are at least bearable.

South African mining authorities are quick to point out that as far as deep mining is concerned, their gold mines have a fairly good safety record. Nor are the black miners alone relegated to the difficult and dangerous tasks. White miners who work side by side with the blacks share both the hardships and the dangers. White South Africans are also extremely proud of the fact that many of the black miners do not come from South Africa itself, but are eager recruits from neighboring black-ruled countries, where wages are much lower than they are for South African black miners.

These statements, while quite true, obscure some vital facts. White miners, no matter what job they do, are paid more than black miners. A white miner can reasonably expect to rise in his position and salary. Black miners always have the lowest jobs, and cannot expect to become foremen, nor dream that their children may one day sit on the board of directors of the mining company. The neighboring countries, from which many of these miners come, do not have the natural wealth of South Africa.

Black miners are not exactly free agents, either. They work under contracts that normally run a year or two. During that time they are housed in barracks, with all their food, medical care, and entertainment—such as it is—provided by the mining company. The movements of black miners are severely restricted by a host of regulations, and of course strikes are unthinkable. The unions, which have only white members, are powerful advocates of keeping the pay and status of black miners down. Any sign of black labor unrest is met quickly and with force by police who are in essence agents of the mining companies.

It is difficult to compare pay scales of black South African miners with those in America or Western Europe, because ways of life are so very different. Black miners receive under one hundred dollars a month. From this is deducted the cost of housing, food, and other services provided by the company, so there is not a great deal of take-home pay by any standard. A miner may work two years in order to save enough to buy a cow in his native village. These are some of the ugly realities that lie behind the beautiful golden ornaments that so many of us crave.

Deep beneath the earth, the gold is blasted from the rock face. The shattered ore is loaded into cars for transport to hoists that take it to the surface. At the mills the ore is pounded and processed into gold, poured into thousand-pound bars and sent to the refinery for further purification.

The thousand-pound bricks that leave the mine are generally 88 percent pure gold. Of the remainder, 9 percent may be silver. Other "impurities" in these bars may be such metals as platinum and palladium, which are actually more valuable than gold itself.

All of the gold from the South African mines is sent

to the Rand Refinery in Germiston, a suburb of Johannesburg. The refinery is owned by an association of all of South Africa's mining companies, and handles more than $5 billion in gold each year. Not surprisingly, security measures at the Rand refinery are about as tight as can be found anywhere in the world. The entire refinery is surrounded by high wire fence and watched constantly by well-trained guards. Inside the refinery are a whole hierarchy of electronic devices that set off alarms. They are so sensitive that a sudden draft, or a wandering mouse, have been known to set them ringing. Every alarm is checked at least twice a month to make sure that there are no malfunctions.

At each stage of the refining process the bars are weighed and marked. The security system is expensive and time-consuming, but it works. There has never been a major theft reported at the Rand Refinery. The refinery is careful about waste as well. Nothing is "left for the sweeper." A loss of only .01 percent a year would amount to $750,000.

Despite all the precautions, the gold moves very rapidly through the refining process. It takes only four days, from the time that the rough bars arrive until they are processed into finished gold and shipped out to London and Zurich, the world's two major gold markets, or to other destinations. The reason for the speed is that whatever gold is being processed is not earning interest in a bank or other financial institution. If the refining process at Rand were slowed down by only one day, it would mean a loss of somewhere around $1.2 million a year to the refinery.

Most of the gold that leaves the Rand Refinery is 99.6 percent pure. It is cast into four-hundred-ounce bars that are packed three together in a plastic box, and bound with wire strapping. The wire cannot be cut without breaking a seal, which immediately indicates that the shipment has been tampered with.

Officially, all of this gold is to go to the South African Reserve Bank in Pretoria. The bank is the only institution authorized to sell South African gold. In fact, most of the gold does not go to the vaults in Pretoria at all. The transactions between the refinery and the bank are paper transactions, and the refinery ships gold directly to foreign customers on orders from the bank. Once again speed is important. The gold goes either by ship to London or plane to Zurich.

A small percentage of the gold from Rand is refined even further, to a level of 99.9 percent purity. Such ultrapure gold is too soft for ordinary use as coins or jewelry, but it has some industrial uses and jewelers who prepare their own gold alloys prefer it.

So, from the single source, the mines of the Republic of South Africa, each year flows approximately 75 percent of the Western world's gold supply. The amount of gold mined each year in Communist countries can only be estimated, for they release no official figures; but it comes nowhere near the amount mined in South Africa alone.

South Africa's forty-five working gold mines produce approximately 24,500,000 fine ounces of gold, or 762 metric tons each year. To get that amount, miners have to hoist and crush some 80 million tons of rock. When refined, a year's supply of South African gold could be put into the back of a medium-sized truck—theoretically at least. In fact, a 762-ton load would flatten any truck ever built.

9

MODERN USES OF GOLD

When one speaks of gold today, the first image that comes to mind (to my mind, anyway) is one of stacks of gleaming gold bars secreted deep within the vaults of a Swiss bank, or some equally exotic and mysterious financial institution. In truth, the majority of gold that is sold in the international gold markets today does wind up in vaults somewhere. We shall hear a good deal more of such gold in later chapters. But not all of the world's gold is hidden away. Some of it is not only displayed, but arrogantly flaunted.

Around one fifth of all the gold that is sold annually goes into what those in the gold trade call industrial

SITE: *Gold bracelet with diamond insets from Cartier.*

uses. The term "industrial" is applied rather broadly, for it includes such areas as jewelry, coins, and medallions, not generally thought of as industrial products. Jewelers are by far the largest industrial users, taking about one third of the industrial gold.

Dentists are also major users of gold. They use some sixty-five tons of gold every year, about 8 or 9 percent of the total that goes for industry. Gold's permanence makes it an unbeatable material for filling cavities. In some countries a gold tooth or two not only make excellent replacements for teeth that are missing, but can be highly visible and valuable status symbols as well.

On the more conventionally industrial side, gold has found increasing use in the electronics industry. Since gold will not rust, corrode, or tarnish, and in addition is a good conductor of electricity, contact points made or coated with gold will remain reliable indefinitely, even in undersea cables or communications satellites orbiting in space.

Gold has been used in ordinary television sets, telephones, and radios. Despite the cost of gold, it is not nearly as expensive to use in these homey items as one might imagine. As we have already pointed out, since gold is extremely ductile and malleable, a tiny bit of it can go an astonishingly long way. This makes it very useful in computers, which require an enormous amount of intricate circuitry. Tiny quantities of gold have been used to replace yards of electric wiring in plastic "printed" circuits and have reduced computer hardware to a manageable size. Such circuits are also far more reliable.

Gold has been used in the space program as a protective sheathing for spaceships and their instruments.

Ground workers who have to deal with highly volatile rocket fuel often wear gold-sheathed suits to protect them from the danger of flash fires. When the space program sent the Pioneer IV probe beyond the solar system, the craft contained a message inscribed on a tablet of gold. The message was placed aboard the craft on the admittedly remote possibility that it might someday be found by an intelligent extraterrestrial species that would be able to recognize and interpret it. The message may have to endure untold years, centuries, even millennia of the unknown conditions of space. The scientists could think of no better material to withstand these rigors than gold.

Kings and princes of past ages would cover the roofs of their palaces or domes of their churches with finely beaten gold. Architects of today can cover skyscrapers with gold if they wish. In 1929 the Richfield Oil Building in Los Angeles was covered with gold. Since that time, golden coverings have been used on many churches, the domes of capital buildings, even on the roofs of some fast-food outlets. Of course, modern technology has developed methods of stretching normally stretchable gold much further. It isn't exactly cheap to cover a dome with gold today, but it doesn't take a king's ransom, either.

Gold Key Drive-Ins in the United States have gold shingled roofs that glitter brilliantly in the sunshine. The shingles are made of porcelain with a twenty-three-carat gold coating that is only five millionths of an inch thick. The twenty-eight story Provident Mutual Society Building in Sydney, Australia, is faced with glass that is coated with twenty-two-carat gold.

When we use a term such as "golden splendor," we

are apt to think of such romantic images as the tomb of Tutankhamen, the court of Louis XIV, or the Grand Seraglio of the Sultan of Turkey. Yet, it is almost certain that gold is more visible today than it has ever been.

At one time golden objects could be owned only by the very wealthy indeed. Today practically everyone owns something made of gold, be it a wedding ring, a pin, a watchband, or more humble objects such as spectacle rims. That brings up an interesting question. How can we afford all of this gold? The answer is that many of these golden objects contain very little gold.

Take, for example, liquid gold, which is really a solution of gold chloride and oil. The amount of gold that actually goes into making liquid gold is infinitesimal. It can be used for painting and printing, and as a touch-up on cheap jewelry.

Rolled gold is generally copper with a very thin layer of gold bonded to the outside. This is the kind of gold often found in such items as spectacle frames, gold watchbands, and cheap jewelry. The gold in rolled gold amounts to less than one twentieth of the total weight of the metal used. If the percentage of gold used is above one twentieth, but still very small, an item may be called gold-filled. Laminated gold is a thin layer of gold laminated onto a less valuable metal such as nickel. This is a material used in many watches.

Perhaps you have a gold ring or some other golden object that became tarnished. Now, gold is not supposed to tarnish. Does that mean that the ring was not really gold? Well, not necessarily, for if an item contains a fairly small percentage of gold—for example, nine-carat gold has only 37.5 percent pure gold in it—it will indeed tarnish. Eighteen-carat gold won't, but it contains twice as much gold. It would be more honest to call a material containing less than 50 percent gold a gold-bearing base metal. But it is unlikely that jewelers will ever do this.

There is nothing illegal or immoral about selling rolled gold, gold fill, or nine-carat gold. What does it matter if cheap jewery tarnishes after a few years, when it has probably gone out of style, anyway? No one expects watchbands or spectacle rims to become family heirlooms. One cannot rationally believe that a pair of five-dollar earrings will last forever. If only high-quality gold could be used in jewelry, there would be much less of it around. Unfortunately, most people are not aware of the literally hundreds of different ways in which gold can be fabricated. When they buy something that is supposed to be gold, at a bargain price, they often think they are getting twenty-four-carat solid gold. Few merchants are going to go out of their way to inform a customer that his gleaming gold-filled watchband contains less than 10 percent gold.

Cheapness is not the only reason for adding other metals to gold. As we have already discussed, pure gold is much too soft to be used in jewelry, and virtually all of the gold that we see is alloyed with other metals. Not only do the alloys harden the surface of gold, they also change its color. A wide variety of colored golds are available, and the demand changes according to the fashion. These exotically colored golds are every bit as much "real" gold as gold that has a golden color.

Green gold has silver plus cadmium and zinc as the alloying agents. White gold can be created by using

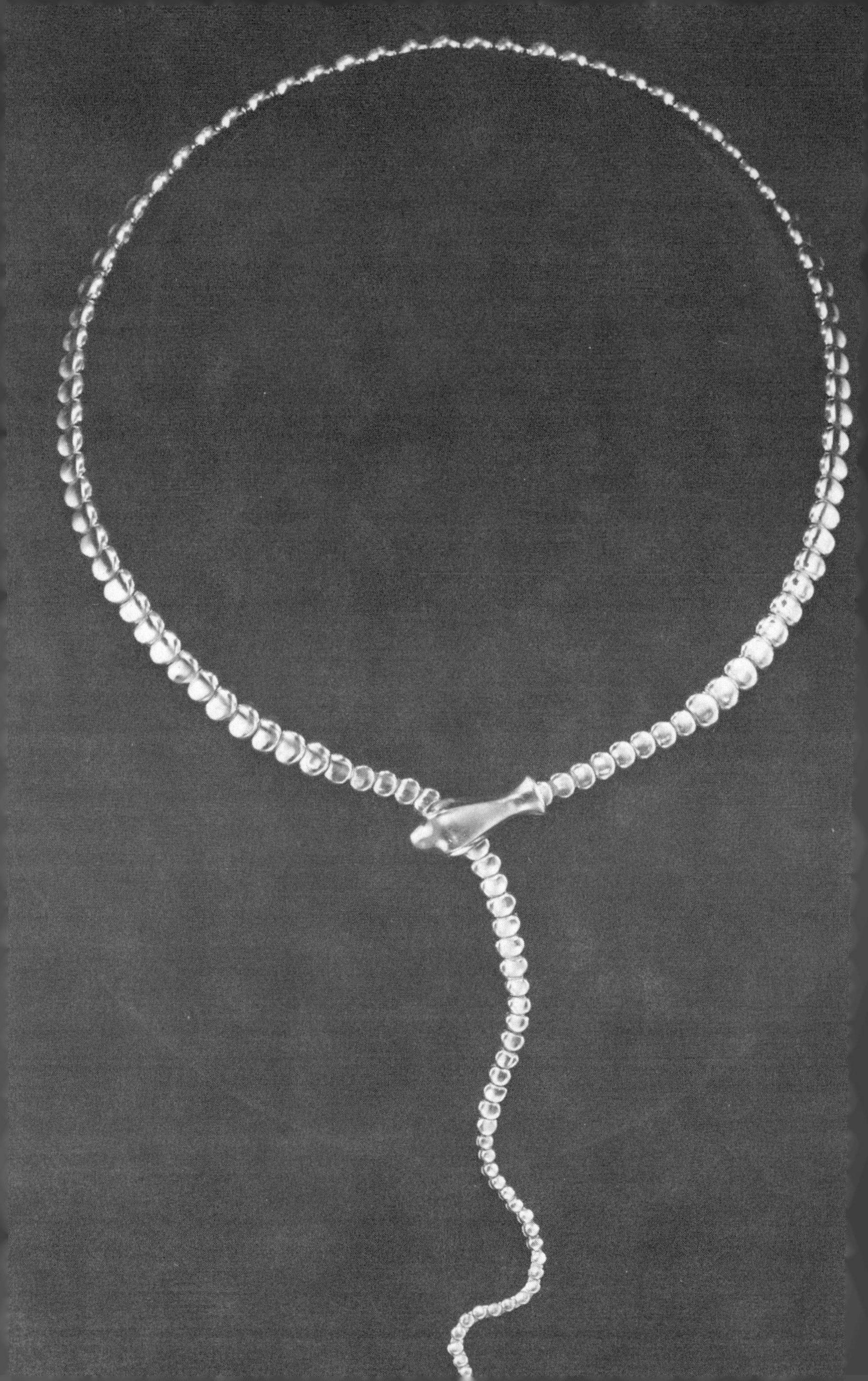

nickel and zinc. Silver and palladium can also be used, but palladium is more expensive than the gold itself, and silver produces a soft gold that still retains a yellowish hue. To get red gold, a little cooper is mixed in, and blue gold contains iron.

Historically, jewelry has been produced by individual craftsmen, working alone or in small shops employing a few skilled artisans. Jewelry making was once the most romantic of crafts. Since the average purchaser had no way of judging the quality of the gold used, he had to rely on the reputation of the craftsmen. Often these craftsmen did their own melting and refining in order to produce just the color and hardness of gold they required. Today much of the jewelry-making business still remains in the hands of individual craftsmen working in small shops. But increasingly mass production has come to dominate the trade. Jewelry making is beginning to look more and more like industry than an art or craft.

Nearly pure gold bars, sold at the London or Zurich markets, are bought by major gold refiners who produce the various sorts of specialized gold demanded by jewelry manufacturers. Very large jewelry-making concerns that have their own refineries buy gold directly. There are fashions and trends in gold, just as there are in clothes, and the successful refiner must be aware of them. There is no point in producing five hundred pounds of fourteen-carat green gold when there are few customers for green gold.

Yellow fourteen-carat gold is most popular in the United States. White gold is also popular, particularly for jewelry set with precious stones, for it is felt that

OSITE: *18 karat gold flexible snake necklace, with jaw that opens* *asten. Designed by Elsa Peretti of Tiffany.*

the pale color sets the stones off more attractively. Red gold is more popular in South America. France and Scandinavia like eighteen-carat gold but with a reddish hue.

The most popular single item of golden jewelry in the United States, and probably in the entire world, is the wedding ring. In the United States a wedding ring is traditionally a simple band of fourteen-carat yellow gold. If you think that the wedding ring, or any other piece of popular jewelry, is hand-crafted in the back of the shop by the jeweler from whom you buy it, you are almost certainly wrong.

More likely it was produced in the factories of a firm such as Italy's Gori & Zucchi. This company is the largest single manufacturer of jewelry in the entire world, and annually consumes around 5 percent of the total of the Western world's new gold production. It began as a small goldsmith's shop, but now the Gori & Zucchi factory in Arezzo employs fifteen hundred people and turns out over six thousand different items ranging from medallions to the plated gold clasps for women's handbags.

Wedding rings are fabricated from fourteen-carat gold wire. This is fed into a machine that spews out finished rings into buckets at a rate too fast for the human eye to follow. The rings and other commonly used gold items are sold by the pound. A large order may include fifty pounds of gold rings, thirty pounds of chain, and a few pounds of brooches.

While gold rings may sell by the pound, manufacturers are not casual about the way gold is treated in their factories. In most of the major jewelry-making plants, security is an obsession. Each workman may be given a measured amount of gold at the start of a day. At the end of the day he must account for every bit of it. There is no such thing as petty pilfering where gold is concerned.

The thought of gold wedding rings being bought and sold by the pound is an unromantic one. But at least a fourteen-carat gold band truly deserves the name, gold, no matter how many of them are manufactured or how. A large percentage of the gold that is used in jewelry fabrication winds up in objects that do not truly deserve the name, gold, at all.

Class rings have always been popular in the United States. Most of them are marked for ten carats, though in fact, they are probably only 9.5 carats. American jewelry is generally half-carat under whatever designation it carries. Anything between 9.5 and 10.5 carats will be labeled ten carats. It should not come as a great surprise to learn that the half-carat leeway is rarely in favor of the customer. As a result, all those ten-carat gold class rings in reality contain between 35 and 40 percent gold. The rest is usually copper. No wonder they begin turning green after a few years. As the price of gold has risen, there has been a trend toward putting less and less gold in cheap "gold" jewelry.

How can you be sure that the piece of jewelry that you buy is actually the quality it is stamped? Unless you have it assayed or tested yourself, you can't be sure. In some countries there is a central assaying office that guarantees the quality of the gold sold in the country. In Britain such an office is run by an ancient organization called the Worshipful Company of Goldsmiths. The Company obtained its first charter in the year 1327, though it had existed for a couple of centuries before that. Gold in Britain may not be sold legally until it has been tested and marked at one of the company's assay offices. Some other European countries have similar systems, or assay offices run directly by the government.

In the United States the jewelry industry is supposed to be self-policing. A variety of consumer-protection laws decree severe penalties for anyone caught mismarking gold. How effective all of this is, is difficult to determine. Undoubtedly, many objects made of gold plate, or gold-bearing base metals, have been sold as genuine eighteen-carat gold. The only advice one can offer about buying expensive gold objects is, know whom you are buying them from. Bargain gold may really turn out to be nothing more than expensive brass.

Still, one is far less likely to be cheated by buying fraudulently marked gold than by simply failing to realize that rolled gold, gold fill, laminated gold, and ten-carat gold are a very long way from being pure gold.

In the past, kings and queens would invest a considerable portion of their wealth in such ornaments as golden crowns. The crowns made an elegant display, of course, but they were also a good investment. In times of trouble, gold crowns and the like would always be melted down and sold. Jewelry as a form of investment had not been popular in the United States until the early 1970s. At that time, with inflation eating away at the value of the dollar, and the price of gold skyrocketing, some people began to advocate using the purchase of gold jewelry as an investment, a hedge against inflation.

While gold may be a good investment sometimes, gold

jewelry rarely is. The markup on jewelry is enormous. A gold ring that sells for fifty or sixty dollars probably cost twenty dollars or less to manufacture. The resale value of most ordinary gold jewelry would be the price of the gold it contained. The average ring is fourteen carats, meaning that only 58 percent of the total weight of the ring is actually gold. In order to simply make back the cost of the ring, the price of gold would have to more than triple above the very high levels it has already reached. Only the most starry-eyed of the gold enthusiasts predict that such a thing will happen, and no knowledgeable gold merchant, no matter how starry-eyed he may be, would advocate using gold jewelry as an investment. Gold bullion, yes, coins perhaps, but never jewelry.

Gold jewelry made by individual craftsmen has even a higher markup than mass-produced jewelry. It may also have a higher resale price, more for its artistic value than the gold it contains. It would be sheer folly to bet on future trends in taste. So, if you buy gold jewelry, you had better buy it because you like it.

The twenty dollar U.S. gold piece, often called the "Double Eagle." (American Numismatic Society)

10

GOOD AS GOLD

When you think about it for a moment, money is both marvelous and mysterious. It is certainly extremely powerful. With a bit of paper and some ink that have no more intrinsic value than the paper and ink used on a page of this book, one can buy the entire book, a bag of groceries, a television set, even an automobile, depending upon the numbers printed on that piece of paper.

People do spend a lot of time thinking about money, but generally in terms of how to get it or what to do with it, not in terms of how and why it works. We may hear vaguely of such things as the International Monetary Fund, or a monetary crisis. We all know about inflation, and that the dollar is worth less now than it used to be, but we don't exactly know how or why. We may also hear of currency devaluation, that international speculators are driving up the price of gold, that the pound is weakening, the lira is collapsing, but the Swiss franc is sound. It's all quite exotic, like catching the fragments of a conversation of a couple of magical adepts discussing powerful rites and symbols about which you know nothing except that they are powerful.

We know that the money system is complicated, but most of us assume that it is rational and based on "solid" or "real" principles, and that it can be understood, if only one took the time and trouble. In our darker moments we may suspect that the secrets are being kept from us, and that the money system is being manipulated by a small group of shadowy figures for their benefit, not ours.

But none of this is really true. Our money system is not rational, solid, or real, as those terms are generally understood. It is an accumulation of traditional practices, beliefs, and even superstitions, as well as private interests, patched together into a system that has not been working very well recently, and that nobody is entirely satisfied with. The system works so long as people believe in it. When they cease believing in it, it doesn't function any more.

Certainly it is possible to understand how the money system works, up to a point, and that there are those who can exercise a considerable degree of control over it. But neither the understanding nor the control are ever perfect. One need only listen to a group of economists discussing a subject such as the causes and cures of inflation to realize that the areas of disagreement are wide and deep. While it is possible, to a degree, to control the flow of money, the system does not always respond predictably. No single small group created the great depression of the 1930s, and no single small group caused the inflation of the 1970s.

Gold has always been important in the money system, and at many times in history gold has been the primary money. In Chapter 3 we discussed how King Croesus of Lydia issued standard gold and silver coins, with a fixed amount of precious metal in each, and a fixed ratio of value between the two. This was called a bimetallic system, meaning simply that two metals were used. The bimetallic system was adopted more or less by most of the other nations of the ancient world.

The Romans perfected the practice of debasing the coinage. They did this by adding more alloy and less precious metal to each coin. The debased coins were stamped with the same value as before, but everyone knew what had been done, and in practice people began to put a lower value on the coins. There were many more coins in circulation, but each coin was worth less. The result was what economists called inflation.

Inflation or no, money was simply too useful to abandon. Throughout the Middle Ages in Europe, gold and silver coins circulated freely. They were issued by different states and sometimes by private individuals. They were of varying quality. People were always looking for easy ways of making money from money. One method was called clipping. Tiny slivers were shaved off the edges of coins. If the slivers were gold they could be valuable, and the metallic value of the clipped coin would be less than it had been previously. To combat this practice, coins were produced with serrated or milled edges. It was then easy to tell if someone had been shaving the edge of the coin. Many coins today are still milled, but that is from custom, for there is no profit to be made by shaving a quarter today.

Another way to get a little extra value out of gold coins was by sweating. The coins would be shaken inside a leather bag, and if shaken hard enough and long enough, some gold dust would be knocked off the coin and collected in the bag. Naturally, people tended to pass on lightweight coins for their face value and hold the heavy coins.

There is a principle in economics called Gresham's law that holds "bad money drives out good money" when there is a fixed rate of exchange between the two. In the case of the coins, the lightweight coins would circulate as everyone tried to pass them on to someone else, while the heavy coins would be held out of circulation as being more valuable. Gresham's law applies to more than coins, and we will come back to it.

Large quantities of gold and silver were heavy as well as risky to carry about. During the Middle Ages, some people would put their gold or silver on deposit with a banker or merchant who would keep the metal in a safe place. The banker or merchant would then issue a note, a piece of paper, that could be redeemed for the amount of gold or silver on deposit. Thus paper money was born.

These promises to pay, or fiduciary money, were originally issued by private individuals or companies as bank notes. Gradually, governments assumed an increasing role in issuing money and by the late eighteenth and early nineteenth centuries, the bulk of money in circulation was paper rather than silver or gold.

But this paper was backed by silver or gold. You could go to a bank or other financial institution and redeem your paper money for the requisite amount of silver or gold. How did anyone know what the requisite amount of gold or silver was? As governments began to take over issuing paper money, they also began to set up their monetary units in terms of fixed weights of both gold and silver. The metal was the standard by which the money was measured. Originally, most European governments tried to establish a bimetallic standard, but it usually degenerated into a monometallic standard in practice. Most governments set too high a value on the silver they coined. Thus, a person who owned gold could go out and buy silver, then bring his silver in to be coined, and make a profit on the deal. It was Gresham's law: The "bad" or cheaper metal, silver, "drove out" the gold. Gold was held and not coined. So most countries were effectively on a silver standard by the early nineteenth century.

But in Britain things had gone differently. Britain followed the advice of Sir Isaac Newton, who, along with being perhaps the greatest scientist that the world has ever known, also served as master of the British Mint. Newton suggested a different relationship between gold and silver: In 1717 gold was overvalued in relation to silver. Britain was, unofficially at least, on a gold standard, though the change wasn't made official until 1816. The United States started on a silver standard but effectively went on the gold standard in 1834. The gold standard in the United States didn't become official until 1900.

In theory at least, when a nation is on a gold standard, it is supposed to keep its currency fully convertible to gold at a fixed rate. For many years a U.S. dollar was worth 23.22 grains of pure gold. A nation should have enough gold in its treasury or financial institutions to convert all the currency back to gold. Therefore, the amount of money in circulation is controlled by the amount of gold.

If the amount of gold increases dramatically, this should have a corresponding effect on the currency. The great gold discoveries in California and Australia in the latter half of the nineteenth century had just such an effect. Gold became more plentiful and the price fell. Very rapidly, gold became the standard monetary metal of the entire Western world, replacing silver.

The system is supposed to regulate itself. If the value of paper currency rises above the value given to gold, then people will trade in their gold for currency. This increases the reserve of gold, and the government can then issue more currency. With more currency in circulation, the value of each unit of currency will fall until it is again on a par with gold.

The reverse is supposed to happen when the value of money falls below that of gold. Then people prefer gold and trade in their money for the metal. The central monetary authorities can then keep currency out of circulation. This produces a scarcity that drives the value of the currency back to its original level on a par with gold.

Though the gold standard was common, not everybody loved it. Throughout the latter half of the nineteenth century, U.S. politics was split by a battle between those who advocated the gold standard and those who wanted more reliance on silver. In addition to the discoveries of gold in the West, silver had also been discovered. If silver were used as a monetary metal, demand would be increased, its value would be raised, and there would be more money in circulation.

In 1896 a thirty-six-year-old Democratic politician from Nebraska named William Jennings Bryan electrified the Democratic presidental convention in Chicago with a speech in which he charged that America was being "crucified on a cross of gold." He was so enthusiastically received that he was swept into the presidential nomination.

Bryan's platform called for the free and unlimited coinage of silver. Bryan and many others thought this would cure the severe economic ills plaguing the small farmer and industrial worker by getting more money into circulation and stimulating the production of silver.

There was still plenty of support for gold in the United States and Bryan lost the presidential election to Republican William McKinley, a conservative gold man. Bryan was renominated two more times by the Democratic party, and remained a power in the party practically until he died in 1925, but after 1900 the free silver issue lost its emotional appeal. Gold had become king, not only in America but throughout the Western world.

The period from about 1900 to the beginning of the First World War marked the great era of the international gold standard. There was, in effect, a single world

Cartoon showing William Bryan, who ran for President three times on a free silver platform, riding a silver dollar. (Culver)

money called by different names in different countries. It was all convertible back to gold at a fixed rate. This was an enormous boon to international trade. With gold always available at a known valuation to settle international debts, importers and exporters could plan ahead and make commitments for the future.

A single gold standard stabilized world currency, since other nations could demand gold instead of currency to settle debts, if the currency of any nation became inflated. Gold would then flow out of a country. Banks and governments seeing their gold reserves decline would want to protect themselves, by reducing the amount of money in circulation. The relationship between gold and currency would once again be brought into balance.

For a while, adjustments of this type took place constantly, and world currency was stabilized. Even today there are some economists and businessmen who look back upon the early years of the twentieth century as a true Golden Age, in every sense of the term. But the gold standard has some big disadvantages. The biggest is that it is very rigid. While it is always possible to print more money, it isn't possible to produce more gold, at least not very quickly. If the price of gold goes up, there will be more incentive to look for gold, or to refine low grade ore, which would have previously been unprofitable. But the expansion of the gold supply is painfully slow. If the price of gold is raised too sharply, it produces instant inflation and economic turmoil. A gold standard does not allow for financial emergencies. It is concerned solely with the stability of the currency.

When a major emergency arose, the machinery of the international gold standard just broke down. That emergency was World War I. As war-threatened governments began selling off their gold to buy armaments, there were more immediate problems than stable currency. A lot of people began buying gold and simply hiding it, assuming that currency was going to lose its value as a result of the war.

When the war was over, currency had indeed lost some of its value. The British pound, the most stable of the international currencies at that time, had lost 10 percent of its value. But the real loser was the German mark. By 1923 it took 1 million paper marks to command a single prewar gold mark. There were tales of people having to take wheelbarrows full of paper marks to buy a loaf of bread. The paper mark, in effect, was no longer worth the paper it was printed on.

Most European nations suspended the gold standard after the war. This meant that currency could no longer be converted to gold. However, the nations also felt that the suspension was just temporary. It had happened before in emergencies. Britain suspended gold convertibility during the Napoleonic Wars. The United States had done so during the Civil War. So, during the 1920s there was a general move back to the international gold standard, but it was never complete or stable. And the system completely broke down once again during the Great Depression of the 1930s.

The United States and the whole of Western Europe were in a financial crisis. Governments whose gold reserves had been badly depleted felt they needed more flexibility to deal with the crisis. Britain went off the gold standard in 1931. In 1932 the election of Franklin D. Roosevelt in the United States put an activist president, and one willing to experiment with economic policies, into the White House. As the crisis of the Depression had deepened, panic-stricken citizens did what they so often do in the face of economic uncertainty; they began exchanging their paper money for gold, and hiding the gold. Foreign investors who held dollars were doing the same thing, and the U.S. gold reserve shrunk from 11 billion to 3.5 billion. Banks were failing as they didn't have the gold, or the cash to meet the demands of depositors who wished to withdraw their assets. One of Roosevelt's first official acts was to declare a bank holiday, so that things could sort themselves out. Most everybody was short of money, and people got along as best they could without cash.

That was only the first step. By the time the banks reopened, in April, 1933, the United States had been taken off the gold standard. The dollar had become what economists call a fiat dollar, a monetary unit enforced on its citizens by a government and accepted by them because they have confidence in the government. The dollar was worth a dollar because the government said it was. The aim was to stimulate the economy by getting more money flowing. The money supply did not have to be limited by the amount of gold.

But this did not mean that gold had suddenly become unimportant. Indeed, the Roosevelt administration moved forcefully to build up the Treasury's dwindling supply of gold. First, foreign shipments of gold were suspended, and then private ownership of gold by U.S. citizens was made illegal. People were ordered to turn in their gold, and certificates entitling them to gold. U.S. citizens could still own nonmonetary gold such as jewelry and antiques.

The ban on foreign shipments of gold was soon lifted and gold was again used in international trade, but the domestic ban remained.

The United States then set out to change the price of gold. It was the first time anyone had tried to manage the price of gold since Isaac Newton had set a price two hundred years earlier. It took a few months to arrive at a price but in January, 1934, President Roosevelt announced that the price of gold would be frozen at thirty-five dollars an ounce. What that meant was that the United States was willing to buy or sell gold at that price.

This represented a considerable increase in price, and it stimulated gold production throughout the world. In 1929 the total annual output of gold had been 19,673,000 fine ounces. In 1936, after the increase in price, it was 35,254,000 fine ounces.

With the official price of gold set at thirty-five dollars an ounce, the dollar was undervalued in relation to gold, and deliberately so. Foreign investors could buy more with a dollar than with one thirty-fifth an ounce of gold, and so foreign nations began trading their gold for dollars. By the end of 1939 the United States had more than half of the world's supply of monetary gold in its vaults.

During this period the Fort Knox Gold Bullion Depository at Fort Knox, Kentucky, became legendary. It was the new Ophir or El Dorado, the place where, at least in the imagination, the bulk of the world's wealth was kept. Fort Knox became a synonym for wealth. Actually, the building itself is a rather unprepossessing granite and concrete structure surrounded by an electrified steel fence. The gold bars are kept within a barren concrete and steel vault, protected by a twenty-ton door. Besides, the bulk of the gold in the United States isn't stored in Fort Knox, and never was. There was and still is generally more gold in the vaults of the New York Federal Reserve Bank on Wall Street. That vault has a ninety-ton door.

Today the Federal Reserve Bank keeps thousands of tons of gold, belonging to some eighty different nations, in its vaults. Often, enormous international financial transactions are carried out within the vault of the Federal Reserve. One nation may wish to make a payment of millions in gold to another. The gold is merely transported on a lift truck, from the cubicle in the vault assigned to the one nation to the cubicle assigned to the other. Transactions that involve shipping large quantities of metal from the bank to some distant point are relatively rare.

There is something totally bizarre and unreal about the whole system. It prompted the Yale economist Professor Robert Triffin to remark:

> Nobody could ever have conceived of a more absurd waste of human resources than to dig gold in distant corners of the earth for the sole purpose of transporting it and reburying it immediately afterward in other deep holes, especially excavated to receive it, and heavily guarded to protect it.

Yet, in a sense, wasteful or not, that is exactly what happens. For years governments have tried to wean people away from gold and into using a more rational and flexible currency system. As we shall see, these attempts have not been entirely successful.

The Second World War provided another shock to the international monetary system. Governments once again poured out their gold reserves to buy armaments. Those private citizens who were rich enough, and frightened enough, bought gold and hid it.

Gold mining in the United States had revived after the gold price was raised, but the U.S. entry into the war stopped mining abruptly. Gold miners were shifted from that industry, which the government considered unessential, to the mining of base metals such as iron that were necessary for the war effort. The ban on gold mining in the United States was lifted in 1946. But mines deteriorate when unworked, and with costs rising while the price of gold stayed the same, few U.S. gold mines reopened, and even fewer stayed in operation. Today the Homestake Mine in South Dakota is the only major U.S. producer of gold.

Realizing that wars inevitably create financial chaos, the allies tried to avert as many problems as possible. When victory seemed in sight, the allied nations sent representatives to an international monetary conference at Bretton Woods, New Hampshire, in 1944.

At the conference an International Bank and the International Monetary Fund (IMF) were set up. The purpose of the IMF was to approve the currency rate of participating countries, and to aid them in keeping their currencies stable by making short-term loans. The real power behind the IMF was the United States, which was incomparably the strongest and wealthiest member. U.S. monetary policy was to have a major effect on the world economy. Currencies were measured not so much in terms of gold, but in terms of U.S. dollars. International faith in the dollar, and to a lesser degree the British pound, was the cornerstone of the new world monetary system.

Gold was still around, of course. The IMF approved the value of most prewar currencies. At first, nations tried to reestablish near-prewar values for their currencies and the currencies were overrated in terms of gold. But most of the currencies were devalued rather quickly. That is, the countries officially recognized the fact that it would take more units of currency, pounds, francs, or whatever to buy an ounce of gold. But the U.S. dollar was fixed at being the equivalent of thirty-fifth an ounce of gold and it subbornly remained there for years, with far-reaching consequences.

John Maynard Keynes, the British economist whose theories were very influential in world economics in the years following World War II, and are still quite influential today, didn't much care for the gold standard. He found it illogical, unreasonable, and too confining; though he didn't advocate doing away with gold entirely as a monetary metal, he did call it a "barbarous relic."

Well, barbarous or not, gold was still there, and still had an important part to play in international finance.

11

THE GOLDBUGS

The London Gold Market is an unlikely-looking place for an international crisis. Indeed, it is an unlikely-looking place for one of the world's major financial clearing houses.

The market is conducted in a small meeting room at the headquarters of N. M. Rothschild & Sons, Ltd., the merchant banking house. The Rothschild family has been in the banking business for over two hundred years. They are one of the most respected (and richest) banking families in the world. In addition to the Rothschild representative, the representatives of four other major gold

ɔSITE: *A workman checks the weight of a gold bar in a London ion firm.* (UPI) bullion dealers sit in the mahogany-paneled room while the market is open.

Each dealer is in touch with his home office through an open telephone line. He knows the price that his own firm is quoting for gold, as well as what is being offered and what is being bid. In front of each dealer is a small British flag. Normally this flag lies on its side. When a dealer puts up his flag or waves it around, that means he wants to stop trading, perhaps to consult with his office. When all the flags are down again, the five representatives get on with the business of fixing the price of gold for the day. The price fixed is a balance between the bids and offers of the five member firms. The London price sets the standard for all international gold sales. It is a very genteel and rather archaic way of doing business. Though the quantities of gold that are bought and sold can be substantial, the gold market isn't very exciting most of the time.

For years the price of gold on the London market had fluctuated within a narrow range of $35.08 to $35.15 an ounce. This remarkable stability was maintained by the fact that everyone knew that ultimately the U.S. Treasury stood ready to either buy or sell gold at $35 an ounce. There was no point in buying or selling for much more or less. That was the value set for U.S. currency in 1934, and maintained ever since. In order to keep this rate, the Treasury had to be ready to go into the market to buy or sell gold, whenever the price threatened to rise or fall from that level.

Then in October, 1960, orders to buy gold began to pour in from all over the world. There were a lot of people with money who were suddenly willing to buy gold for more than $35.15 an ounce. The price rapidly rose to $40 an ounce, an absolutely unheard of figure at the time.

There was to be a presidential election in November. The buying spree had been set off by rumors that the next U.S. president, no matter who he would be, was going to devalue the dollar. That meant that instead of buying and selling for $35 an ounce, the U.S. Treasury might be buying and selling for a higher figure, say, $41 an ounce. Anyone who stocked up on gold at a lower price stood to make an enormous profit.

This particular buying panic collapsed when the United States announced emphatically that it was not going to devalue the dollar, and would maintain the $35 price at all costs. But the events of October, 1960, were just a ripple compared to the waves that were to come later.

What had happened to upset the tranquility of the London Gold Market? The United States had emerged from World War II with the strongest economy and the strongest currency in the world. Until 1949, dollars were still preferred to gold, and gold continued to flow into the vaults at Fort Knox and other U.S. gold depositaries. In that year the United States owned about three quarters of all the monetary gold in the world. It was the high point for U.S. gold reserves. Then, slowly, the flow began to reverse as other countries began cashing in dollars for gold.

The gold drain was barely noticed at first, and for a long time no one worried about it. It seemed a normal balancing of the world's gold supply. With or without gold in Fort Knox, the dollar was still strong because the value of the dollar was guaranteed by the U.S. government. The dollar was backed by the strength of the entire American economy. But starting around 1958, people began to lose confidence in the dollar itself. Throughout the 1940s and early 1950s, if someone wanted to describe something as being strong and unshakable, he might say it was "sound as a dollar." That expression was heard less and less frequently as time went on.

Why had people begun to lose confidence in the dollar? There is no simple answer to that question; indeed, there is no answer, simple or complicated, that everyone would agree upon.

America had spent a great deal of money abroad in the years between 1944 when the IMF was established and 1960 when trouble began to show up on the gold market. The Marshall Plan for the reconstruction of Western Europe was expensive, and so was the Korean War. The war with Germany and Japan was over but the cold war with Russia was on, and defense expenditures remained high. There were expenses at home as well. Vast quantities were being spent on highways and other public works projects, and on social welfare programs. Later, there was to be the long, and extremely costly, war in Southeast Asia. The U.S. economy wasn't expanding fast enough to support all of these expenses. The national debt climbed steeply.

The United States was no longer as economically or politically dominant as it had been at the end of World War II. There was competition, not only from Communist countries but from other Western countries as well. Americans started buying Japanese cameras and German cars. People began to get the idea that there were too many dollars around, and that the United States didn't have the gold, or the economic strength to back them up completely. Other European currencies, most particularly the British pound, were also affected.

The depletion of U.S. gold reserves did not create the problems of the dollar. It probably contributed to the problems, though to what degree is a matter of considerable dispute. The gold drain was certainly symbolic of the problems. But one fact that is beyond dispute is that when people begin to lose confidence in currency they turn, as they always have, to gold. This pushes up the price of gold, which contributes to uneasiness about currency, which pushes up the price of gold again, and so on. It is a self-feeding cycle.

The years following 1960 saw a resurrection of that financial figure known as the goldbug. They might prefer to call themselves sound money advocates, but the term goldbug is the one that has stuck. These individuals lack faith in the world economy as it is now structured. They would probably prefer a return to the full gold standard, but they know such a return is unlikely. So, to protect their own wealth from the decline and collapse that they fear is inevitable, they invest in gold, either bars of gold that are sold on the London or other gold exchanges, gold coins, or gold mining stocks.

The goldbug contends that the gold standard imposes a much-needed restraint on government spending. If the government can print no more money than it has gold to back that money, then the government cannot go into debt, no matter how worthwhile the cause may seem. But the goldbug distrusts governments almost as much

Financiers Jay Gould (seated right) *and Jim Fisk* (seated left) *plot to corner the U.S. gold market in 1869.* (Culver)

as he distrusts paper currency, and assumes that governments will never stop spending until the money system collapses. The only safety for the individual then is to buy gold, no matter what effects the flight of a large quantity of money into gold would be. At its core, the philosophy of the goldbug is one of unabashed self-interest. The goldbug assumes everyone acts out of self-interest, only he is being a bit more clever.

The actions of the goldbug have often been frowned upon by other financial figures. If you invest in stocks and bonds, the money ultimately goes into the production of products that presumably result in the creation of more wealth. But gold doesn't do anything. It just sits there in the vault, where it must be guarded. Of course, gold has industrial uses, and can be sold for that purpose, but the only way to really make money on gold is for the world economy to go downhill. Goldbugs are always predicting this, and doomsayers rarely win popularity contests. Buying gold in quantity tends to weaken currencies, and accelerate economic decline. The goldbugs have often been accused of engaging in self-fulfilling prophecies of economic disaster. By their own manipulations goldbugs are sometimes able to bring about the financial crises out of which they can make an enormous profit.

Unscrupulous manipulation of the gold market is nothing new. A little over a century ago an American financial buccaneer named Jay Gould, through a combination of conspiracy and bribery managed to buy up most of the gold available in the U.S. gold market. Others jumped on the Gould-created bandwagon, and the price of gold shot upward. Gould knew that as soon as the price of gold hit a certain level, the government would begin selling part of its gold reserve to maintain the price level. But others didn't know this. Gould quietly sold out after making a fantastic profit, and just before the announcement came through that the government was selling gold. The price of gold plummeted. Hundreds of firms and thousands of investors were wiped out. The day on which all of this happened —Friday, October 4, 1869—was known as Black Friday from then on.

Today there is a suspicion, probably a correct one, that there is a lot of dirty and illegal money in gold. Many dictators bought large quantities of gold and stored it away in Swiss banks, or other institutions that guard the identity of their depositors. Many Americans—though it was illegal to own gold—avoided taxes by anonymously squirreling their hordes away in Swiss banks. Money made from criminal activity, anything from illegal stock manipulation to the international drug trade, can buy gold to be hidden in the concrete vaults of the banks of Zurich. In short, if one wants to hide a large quantity of money safely, gold is a good way to do it.

Between 1954 and 1957, most of the gold sold in the international markets was sold to central banks buying gold for their monetary reserves. But, since 1957, the majority of gold has gone into private hands; some of it is used for industrial purposes, but the largest percentage goes to the goldbugs.

The price of gold-mining stocks generally goes up when the price of gold itself rises, and goldbugs like gold stocks almost as much as the refined stuff. But the relationship between the price of gold and the profitability of gold stocks is not always clear. Many of the major mining groups also have investments in other areas, so at least some of the profits and losses come from products other than gold. An investment in a mining concern that makes a rich find can yield profits considerably in excess of those one might get by investing in gold alone. On the other hand, the failure of a mine could result in a major loss for a gold stock even if the price of gold is going up. *Wall Street Journal* writer Ray Vicker calls gold stocks "a left-handed way of investing in gold."

The goldbugs became increasingly active after the 1960 flurry. Every world crisis or rumor of trouble was followed by a wave of gold buying, and an additional drain of the gold stockpiles of the United States and her primary financial partner, Britain. A variety of attempts were made to keep the gold price at thirty-five dollars an ounce. First the London Gold Pool was formed, with the Bank of England acting as agent for nations belonging to the pool. American monetary authorities and six European central banks agreed to intervene in the gold market when necessary. If the price started to rise above thirty-five dollars an ounce, the pool would release gold from the vast horde stored by the cooperating nations. It was hoped that the mere contemplation of $30 billion or so in gold available to the pool would discourage speculators. It didn't.

You might wonder what nations like the Soviet Union and China did while all this frantic gold excitement was going on. Indeed, the Soviet Union has an active gold-mining industry. It is, second to South Africa, the world's largest gold producer, though total production is only a fraction that of South Africa. Also, the Soviets are very secretive about the amount of gold they produce. In 1974 the entire Eastern European bloc sold 7.2 million fine ounces of gold on the international market. That was way behind South Africa's 24.5 million fine ounces, but ahead of the United State's 1.125 million fine ounces.

It is presumed that the Soviets have a considerable stockpile of gold, and from time to time there are rumors that the Soviets are going to dump a lot of gold on the market in order to create economic chaos in the West. In fact, the Soviets have been very conservative about the way they have used gold. Dumping a large quantity of gold on the market would simply depress the price, and they would be the losers. The Chinese, though their gold supplies are much smaller, have also used them with caution.

By the end of 1967, the British were forced to devalue the pound. International money men decided that Britain no longer had the economic strength to support the pound at its set value. They began trading in pounds for gold or other currencies. That forced the devaluation. Next to the dollar, the pound had been the cornerstone of the monetary system established in 1944 at Breton Woods. The system, which had never worked very well, anyway, was beginning to break down completely.

During the first weeks of 1968 there was a genuine gold-buying panic. Orders poured into London from places like Singapore, Geneva, and Beirut. The London market had once traded eighteen tons of gold in a good week; now it was trading eighteen tons a day. The Gold Pool kept pouring in reserves. The United States lost $2 billion in gold and the other Gold Pool members pumped in another billion. But the pressure of the goldbugs did not abate.

Something had to give, and on March 14, 1968, the Gold Pool was dissolved, and with the cooperation of the International Monetary Fund, what is called a two-tier price for gold was established. What this meant was that banks acting as agents for their governments were still able to buy gold at the established thirty-five dollars an ounce price, but everyone else could buy gold on a free market, where the price of gold would find its own level.

The London Gold Market was then closed for the remainder of the month, hopefully to allow things to cool down a bit. The goldbugs, however, were in no mood to cool down. Banks in Zurich recognized there was still a big demand for gold and they were ready to take advantage of it. They formed their own gold pool, made contact with South Africa to purchase gold, and opened a gold market in Zurich. The price was set between forty-three and forty-five dollars an ounce, and there were plenty of buyers at that price. Zurich quickly replaced London as the world center for gold marketing.

Virtually everybody in world finance knew that the two-tier gold market was nothing but a stopgap measure. Monetary authorities hoped that the spread between the thirty-five dollars an ounce price and the free market price would not grow to more than seven or eight dollars, so that the compromise could be kept going until something better could be agreed upon. Across the world people continued to buy gold.

By August of 1971, the U.S. gold reserves had sunk to the dangerously low level of $10 billion, while foreign claims against the dollar totaled $43 billion. If every non-American who held a dollar, or even half their number, had tried to cash in their dollars for gold, the result would have been chaos.

By the end of 1971, chaos seemed at hand. President Richard Nixon made a whole series of dramatic economic moves, including a freeze on domestic wages and prices. He also severed all the remaining official links that the U.S. dollar had with gold. In December, 1971, there was a major international monetary conference held at Washington's Smithsonian Institution. The U.S. government announced that it was going to do something that a whole series of U.S. administrations, Republican and Democratic, swore that they never were going to do. The dollar was to be devalued. The price was set at thirty-eight dollars an ounce of gold rather than the thirty-five dollars that had been the price since 1934. But the gold traders set the value of the dollar even lower. On the free market gold was constantly selling at above forty-two dollars an ounce, and going up.

There was yet another monetary crisis in January and February of 1973, and the dollar was devalued again by another 10 percent. But the price of gold kept right on going up until, by the end of 1973, the price had reached an incredible $198 an ounce. Remember, just five years before the price had been thirty-five an ounce.

Goldbugs were predicting that the price of gold would rise to three hundred dollars an ounce or more. But it never reached those dizzying heights, for reasons that we will discuss in the next chapter. In the meantime, however, Americans who had been accustomed to regarding the dollar as being as good as gold, or better, were taking a new look.

In countries where currency has traditionally been unstable, or where people are simply unused to paper money, gold hoarding has always been a tradition. In India, one of the poorest countries in the world, practically every household, no matter how poor, has some small cache of gold. To the Indian peasant, gold has an almost religious significance, and many superstitions are attached to it. Wearing gold is supposed to promote fertility, and some gold is part of practically every Indian woman's dowry. It has a more practical purpose as well. In a land of recurrent famines, gold can be traded for food in hard times, when currency is no longer good enough or when there is no currency available. When so much wealth is tied up in a material that is simply hidden away somewhere, this creates financial problems even in wealthy lands. The Indian government had made gold hoarding illegal, but to no avail. The traditional attachment to gold has been stronger than any law. Gold smuggling is a major industry in India.

The ownership of gold in the United States, aside from jewelry or antiques, had been illegal since 1934, and gold hoarding had never been much of a problem, until the 1970s. There were always a few odd eccentrics who kept illegal gold hidden in their cellars or attics or buried in their backyards because they didn't trust paper money or banks. There is a persistent rumor, and perhaps a true one, of a huge illegal gold horde hidden away somewhere in the West in an area that was later to become a nuclear testing ground. The owner of this illegal gold, so it is said, is trying to negotiate selling the gold to the government without incurring any legal penalties for owning it in the first place.

Though it was still illegal for U.S. citizens to own gold even abroad, an increasing number bought and stored gold in Switzerland. Swiss banks display gold bars of all sizes and shapes right in their windows. These can be purchased and then stored in the bank with no questions asked. Such purchases are hard to trace and Swiss bankers are not cooperative. As uncertainty about the soundness of the dollar grew and the price of gold went up, so did illegal gold hoarding among Americans, both in the United States and abroad.

Aside from jewelry, which, as already mentioned, costs much more than its bullion value, there was another perfectly legal form in which Americans could hold gold. It was in the form of gold coins.

Most of the countries of the world, including the United States, once minted gold coins for circulation and for many years they were used in ordinary commerce. The most popular U.S. gold coin was the twenty-dollar double eagle. The twenty-dollar double eagle is no longer being minted, and cannot be used as legal tender. It would be foolish to try because the coin is worth a lot more than twenty-dollars today. The same is true of most other gold coins. But, in some parts of the world, gold coins are still used for the payment of debts. For example, when Egypt supported a revolt in Yemen during the early 1960s, it was paying the armies of the side that it backed in gold sovereigns, a gold coin once minted in Britain. The tribesmen of Yemen, which had once been under British rule, knew the coin and trusted it. The other side in the Yemen civil war was also using gold sovereigns.

A large percentage of coins such as the twenty-dollar double eagles and the sovereigns that are around today are actually counterfeit. Until the recent civil war, Lebanon was the world center for counterfeit gold coins. It was perfectly legal in Lebanon to counterfeit the coins of other countries. What was done with them after they were minted was of no concern to a tolerant Lebanese government. Making gold coins was an odd sort of counterfeiting, though, for the fake coins almost always contained the same weight of gold as the originals. The Lebanese coin makers didn't short-weight the gold because they wanted repeat customers. These gold counterfeiters—rather than trying to sell fake coins—were actually selling gold in a popular and familiar form. It was a profitable business and most of the coin buyers neither knew nor cared whether the sovereigns they purchased were minted in Britain in 1912 or in Beirut in 1971, just so long as they contained the proper amount of gold.

U.S. coin collectors were allowed to keep gold coins as collectors' items. As the price of gold went up a lot of noncollectors began buying gold coins, just so they could legally possess gold. The coins were cheaper and more reliable than jewelry.

The price of gold coins, many of them counterfeit and thus without real numismatic or coin collection value, rose sharply. U.S. coin buyers, while obeying the letter of the law against private gold holdings, were certainly violating its spirit.

Hard-core goldbugs had been predicting the collapse of the world monetary system ever since the gold standard was abandoned, and their voices grew louder and more strident during the early 1970s. The only thing you could trust in the uncertain financial world was gold. There were predictions that the price of gold would rise to three hundred dollars an ounce or even four hundred dollars, while the paper dollar would become valueless. Not only would there be financial chaos, said the more extreme goldbugs, there would be political and social chaos as well.

In a very popular book of the early seventies, the author advised his readers to buy a cabin in some remote and inaccessible place, stock it with canned goods, buy as many gold coins as possible, and then buy a gun with which you can protect your horde of food and gold from marauders. The author said he already had his cabin, canned goods, sacks of gold coins, and his gun. He was ready to hide out as soon as the money system fell apart and hungry mobs began roaming the streets trying to buy food with worthless dollars. He must have been able to build up his stock of gold coins considerably with the royalties from his best-selling book and fees from the many lectures he gave. How many actually followed his advice is unknown. There may be hundreds of cabins stocked with canned goods and gold coins out there somewhere.

This particular bit of doomsaying was extreme even for the chronically pessimistic goldbugs. Or, was it? A lot of people still remembered what had happened in Germany in the 1920s when paper money lost all its value, and only gold could purchase food. Goldbugs had attained a new respectability.

The *Wall Street Journal* recognized the new respectability of the goldbug philosophy in a front-page story on February 8, 1974:

The "gold bugs" are flying high. Once pesky pariahs on Wall Street for their stubborn insistence that gold rather than cash or the stock market is the only source of true wealth, the gold fanciers have suddenly become respectable. Says Harry Schultz, publisher of a London-based newsletter on gold: "No more are we nut-cases, kooks, antediluvians, weirdoes, crackpots, and dreamers."

While all currencies and most securities have taken a drubbing in the past few years, gold and gold-mining stocks have rocketed in price. Now just about everybody seems to be scurrying to get a piece of the action.

12

THE GOLDEN FUTURE

At the beginning of 1975 the prohibition against Americans owning gold was finally lifted. For the first time since 1934, U.S. citizens were able to go out and legally buy bars of gold to put in their bank vaults, or in their basements, if they so desired. The end of the gold ban had been announced well in advance. Goldbugs confidently predicted that Americans in enormous numbers would be anxious to trade in their increasingly valueless paper money for some of the precious yellow stuff. Some gold dealers expected a new gold rush. But it never happened.

Modest numbers of people came in to buy gold. Some

...SITE: *Mary Brooks, former director of the mint, shows gold bars* ...*e U.S. bullion depository at Fort Knox, Kentucky.* (UPI) buyers doubtless regarded gold as the only secure investment in an increasingly insecure world. Others bought it for the sheer romantic joy of owning some of the fabled substance in its pure or near-pure form. Gold still sells in the United States today, but in nowhere near the quantities that the goldbugs had predicted.

Before the gold sale in the United States, the price of gold had actually been declining. The gold price had stood at above $190 an ounce at the end of 1974. By mid-1975 the average price had gone down to about $160 an ounce, and it kept right on declining through the rest of 1975 and into 1976. By April, 1976, the price of gold was in the $120 to $130 an ounce range. Suddenly gold was not looking like such a great investment any more. Fortunes had been made when the price of gold shot up. Now some of those fortunes were being whittled down, and for the speculator who bet on a price rise in 1975 similar to the one that had occurred in 1974, the fall in price may have meant financial disaster.

The gold price rose slightly in anticipation of a wave of gold buying in America, but when that wave failed to materialize, the price began dropping again.

What had happened? Actually, something had failed to happen: The entire economic system of the United States and allied Western nations did not collapse. It was the specter of economic anarchy that provided much of the emotional force behind the gold buying spree of 1973 and 1974.

In fact, instead of collapsing, the economic picture actually seemed to be improving. Inflation, one of the elements most responsible for people losing faith in paper currency, was slowing down. The deep economic recession into which the United States had slipped showed signs of letting up. The economies of other Western countries were improving as well. The war in Southeast Asia had ended and war in the Middle East had been averted, for the time being.

For those who had loose cash lying about, there were other places to invest it for a quick return. The stock market had shown signs of improvement by mid-1975. There were predictions of a booming, money-making market in the beginning of 1976. These predictions turned out to be spectacularly correct, as the market had its greatest rise in history during January of 1976.

The picture wasn't entirely rosy. It never is. The economic optimism might collapse any time now for a variety of reasons. The doom cryers could be back in the streets telling people to grab their gold and head for their cabins in the hills. But, for the moment at least, the specter has been banished, and gold, the magic talisman, seems somehow less necessary, less attractive.

There were more technical reasons for gold's fall from grace. For years now the Internal Monetary Fund has been trying to phase out gold as a primary medium of international commerce by developing some sort of system of international money.

The IMF developed a plan that it hopes will fill this need. The system has the uninspiring name of Special Drawing Rights (SDR). Since SDR is to be used only in international transactions, it has been given the nickname, "paper gold." But it isn't gold, and it isn't even really paper. It is just a bookkeeping entry in the IMF books, in which credit from one member nation is transferred to another.

Originally, the percentage of SDR each nation was to be credited with depended on the amount of gold and currency the nation had deposited with the IMF. The amount of SDR each nation could use was greater than the gold or currency on deposit. It was a form of international credit. SDR were meant to supplement gold in international monetary affairs, mainly because there just wasn't enough gold around. World trade had increased faster than the gold supply, and what new gold there was was quickly disappearing into the vaults of hoarders. This presented a major stumbling block to commerce.

Economists like John Maynard Keynes had been trying to get gold out of the money system for over half a century. When the United States severed the link between gold and the dollar in 1971, the world monetary system agreed on at the end of World War II and partially dependent on gold, had died. Something was needed to replace it.

In January of 1974 a prestigious group called the Committee of Twenty, which represents the nations affiliated with the IMF, met to consider a restructuring of the world monetary system. One of the reforms the committee decided on was that the value of SDR should no longer be tied to gold. How the value of SDR was to be determined was based on a complicated formula that does not really concern us here. We are talking about gold, and the formula excluded gold.

At one time such a decision might have brought about a near-panic in the gold market. It meant that there should have been less of a demand for gold, for nations would no longer have to store huge quantities of gold in their vaults for international trade. The price of gold should have dropped. But no one in the gold market paid much attention to the committee's decision, and the price of gold rose higher than ever before during 1974.

But, in August of 1975 when the IMF actually began getting rid of its stock of 153 million ounces of gold, the reaction was quite different. The price of gold had already been falling, and the IMF announcement caused another 10 dollars an ounce drop in the price on the London market.

A nonmonetary factor that led to the weakening of gold prices during 1975 was a slackening of industrial demand. The industrial demand for gold had been rising steadily for years, but at $198 an ounce gold was just too expensive. Users from electronics manufacturers to dentists began cutting back and substituting, as best they could, other materials. As the price of gold fell throughout 1975, industrial demand rose once again.

Friedrick Engels, friend and collaborator of Karl Marx, had once remarked that a day would come when gold would be used for toilet seats. That puts the matter a bit crudely but makes a point. Will the time come when gold no longer has any special significance, when it will be used, if not for toilet seats, then primarily as an electrical conductor or in tooth fillings? Silver, once an important monetary metal, is now used almost entirely for industrial purposes. If gold is officially phased out of the money system, will it lose its special significance, and be treated only as a scarce metal with some uncommon and useful characteristics?

Somehow that seems extremely doubtful. The human race has had a very special relationship with gold for thousands and thousands of years. History and tradition have given it an emotional, almost mystical, significance that far transcends whatever practical value it possesses as a useful metal. Gold has been the symbol of divinity, immortality, and royalty. In more recent times it has been the unparalleled symbol of financial stability.

In our modern, highly sophisticated, highly complex economy, millions still reacted with primordial emotions when economic troubles threatened. They began hoarding gold. When the next crisis comes, they are likely to react the same way, whether gold is part of the money system or not. There is simply no other material that matches the ancient and universal respect in which gold is held. Habits that are thousands of years old are hard to break.

Whether we call it money or not, gold is likely to remain—well, gold.

SELECTED BIBLIOGRAPHY

ALLEN, GINA. *Gold Is.* New York: Meredith Press, 1969.
BARLETT, RICHARD A. *The New Country.* New York: Oxford U. Press, 1974.
BURLAND, C. A. *The Arts of the Alchemist.* New York: Macmillan, 1967.
CERAM, C. W. *Gods, Graves and Scholars.* New York: Knopf, 1951.
———. *Hands On the Past.* New York: Knopf, 1966.
CHAPMAN, WALKER. *The Search for El Dorado.* New York: Bobbs-Merrill, 1967.
DESROCHES-NOBLECOURT, Christiane. *Tutankhamen.* New York: N.Y. Graphic Society, 1963.
EINZING, PAUL. *The Destiny of Gold.* London: Macmillan, 1972.
GODWIN, JOHN. *This Baffling World.* New York: Hart Publishing, 1968.
GRANT, MICHAEL. *The Army of the Caesars.* New York: Scribners, 1974.
———. *Cleopatra.* New York: Simon and Schuster, 1972.
HAWKES, JACQUETTA (ed.). *The World of the Past* (2 vols.). New York: Knopf, 1963
HELMYARD, E. J. *Alchemy.* Baltimore, Md.: Penguin, 1957.
HEMMING, JOHN. *The Conquest of the Incas.* New York: Harcourt Brace, 1970.
INNES, HAMMOND. *The Conquistadors.* New York: Knopf, 1969.
JULY, ROBERT W. *A History of the African People.* New York: Scribners, 1970.
READ, JOHN. *Prelude to Chemistry.* Cambridge, Mass.: M.I.T. Press, 1968.
ROBINSON, FAYETTE, and STREET, FRANKLIN. *The Gold Mines of California.* New York: Promontory Press, 1974.
VICKER, RAY. *The Realms of Gold.* New York: Scribners, 1975.

INDEX